new interchange

English for international communication

Jack C. Richards

with Jonathan Hull and Susan Proctor

student's book

1

New Interchange Student's Book revision prepared by Jack C. Richards.

CAMBRIDGE
UNIVERSITY PRESS

PUBLISHED BY THE PRESS SYNDICATE OF THE UNIVERSITY OF CAMBRIDGE
The Pitt Building, Trumpington Street, Cambridge, United Kingdom

CAMBRIDGE UNIVERSITY PRESS
The Edinburgh Building, Cambridge CB2 2RU, UK
40 West 20th Street, New York, NY 10011–4211, USA
477 Williamstown Road, Port Melbourne, VIC 3207, Australia
Ruiz de Alarcón 13, 28014 Madrid, Spain
Dock House, The Waterfront, Cape Town 8001, South Africa

http://www.cambridge.org

First published 1997
First edition packaged with audio CD 2001
7th printing 2003

New Interchange Student's Book 1 has been developed from *Interchange* Student's Book 1,
first published by Cambridge University Press in 1990.

Printed in Hong Kong, China
Typeface New Century Schoolbook *System* QuarkXPress® [AH]
A catalog record for this book is available from the British Library

Library of Congress Cataloging in Publication data
Richards, Jack C.
New interchange: English for international communication :
student's book 1 / Jack C. Richards with Jonathan Hull and Susan Proctor.
p. cm.
Rev. ed. of: Interchange : English for international communication :
student's book 1. 1990.
ISBN 0-521-62881-4
1. English language – Textbooks for foreign speakers.
2. Communication, International – Problems, exercises, etc.
I. Hull, Jonathan. II. Proctor, Susan. III. Richards,
Jack C. Interchange. IV. Title.
PE1128.R459 1997
428.2'4 – dc21 97-17432
CIP

ISBN 0 521 00057 2 Student's Book 1 w/audio CD
ISBN 0 521 62880 6 Student's Book 1A
ISBN 0 521 62879 2 Student's Book 1B
ISBN 0 521 62878 4 Workbook 1
ISBN 0 521 62877 6 Workbook 1A
ISBN 0 521 62876 8 Workbook 1B
ISBN 0 521 62875 X Teacher's Edition 1
ISBN 0 521 62874 1 Teacher's Manual 1
ISBN 0 521 62873 3 Class Audio Cassettes 1
ISBN 0 521 62871 7 Student's Audio Cassette 1A
ISBN 0 521 62869 5 Student's Audio Cassette 1B
ISBN 0 521 62872 5 Class Audio CDs 1
ISBN 0 521 62870 9 Student's Audio CD 1A
ISBN 0 521 62868 7 Student's Audio CD 1B
ISBN 0 521 65913 2 Audio Sampler 1–3

Also available
ISBN 0 521 62867 9 Video 1 (NTSC)
ISBN 0 521 62866 0 Video 1 (PAL)
ISBN 0 521 62865 2 Video 1 (SECAM)
ISBN 0 521 62864 4 Video Activity Book 1
ISBN 0 521 62863 6 Video Teacher's Guide 1
ISBN 0 521 63887 9 Video Sampler 1–2
ISBN 0 521 62667 6 CD-ROM (PC format)
ISBN 0 521 62666 8 CD-ROM (Mac format)
ISBN 0 521 62882 2 New Interchange/Passages Placement and Evaluation Package
ISBN 0 521 80575 9 Teacher-Training Video with Video Manual

Book design, art direction, and layout services: Adventure House, NYC
Illustrators: Adventure House, Barbara Griffel, Randy Jones, Mark Kaufman, Kevin Spaulding, Sam Viviano
Photo researcher: Sylvia P. Bloch

Introduction

THE NEW EDITION

New Interchange is a revision of *Interchange*, one of the world's most successful and popular English courses. *New Interchange* incorporates many improvements suggested by teachers and students from around the world. Some major changes include many new Conversations, Snapshots, and Readings; more extensive Grammar Focus models and activities; a greater variety and amount of listening materials; extensive changes to the **Teacher's Edition** and **Workbook**; and additions to the **Video.**

New Interchange is a multi-level course in English as a second or foreign language for young adults and adults. The course covers the four skills of listening, speaking, reading, and writing, as well as improving pronunciation and building vocabulary. Particular emphasis is placed on listening and speaking. The primary goal of the course is to teach communicative competence, that is, the ability to communicate in English according to the situation, purpose, and roles of the participants. The language used in *New Interchange* is American English; however, the course reflects the fact that English is the major language of international communication and is not limited to any one country, region, or culture. This level is for beginners and takes students from the beginning to low-intermediate level.

This level builds on the foundations for accurate and fluent communication already established in the prior level by extending grammatical, lexical, and functional skills. Because the syllabus covered in this Student's Book reviews language features taught at the prior level, students who have not previously used *New Interchange* can successfully study at this level.

COURSE LENGTH

Each full level of *New Interchange* contains between 70 and 120 hours of class instruction time. For classes where more time is available, the Teacher's Edition gives detailed suggestions for Optional Activities to extend each unit. Where less time is available, the amount of time spent on Interchange Activities, Reading, Writing, Optional Activities, and the Workbook can be reduced.

Each split edition contains approximately 35 to 60 hours of classroom material. The Student's Book, Workbook, and Student's Audio Cassettes or CDs are available in split editions.

COURSE COMPONENTS

The **Student's Book** contains 16 six-page units, each divided into two topical/functional "cycles," as well as four review units. At the back of the book are 16 communication tasks, called "Interchange Activities," and summaries of grammar and vocabulary taught in each unit.

The full-color **Teacher's Edition** features detailed teaching instructions directly across from the Student's Book pages, along with audio scripts, cultural notes, answer keys, and optional activities. At the back of the Teacher's Edition are instructions for Interchange Activities, an Optional Activities Index, a Workbook Answer Key, and four photocopiable Achievement Tests with audio scripts and answer keys.

The **Workbook** provides a variety of reading, writing, and spelling exercises to reinforce the grammar and vocabulary taught in the Student's Book. Each six-page unit follows the same teaching sequence as the Student's Book; some exercises recycle teaching points from previous units in the context of the new topic. The Workbook can be used for classwork or homework.

The **Class Audio Program**, available on cassette or CD, is intended for classroom use. The Conversations, Grammar Focus models, Pronunciation exercises, and Listening activities in the Student's Book are all recorded naturally with a variety of native and some nonnative accents. Recorded exercises are indicated with the symbol .

The **Student's Audio Program** provides opportunities for self-study. It contains recordings of all Student's Book exercises marked with the symbol , except for the Listening tasks, which are intended only for classroom use. These tasks appear exclusively on the Class Audio Program and are indicated by the symbol CLASS AUDIO ONLY.

The **Video** offers entertaining dramatic or documentary sequences that review and extend language learned in each unit of the Student's Book. The **Video Activity Book** contains comprehension, conversation, and language practice activities, and the **Video Teacher's Guide** provides instructional support, answer keys, and photocopiable transcripts of the video sequences.

The **CD-ROM**, appropriate for home or laboratory use, offers a wealth of additional practice. Each of the 16 units is based on a sequence from the Video. Four tests help students monitor their progress.

The **Placement Test** helps determine the most appropriate level of *New Interchange* for incoming students. A booklet contains the four-skills test on photocopiable pages, as well as instructions for test administration and scoring. A cassette accompanies the listening section of the test.

The **Lab Cassettes** provide self-study activities in the areas of grammar, vocabulary, pronunciation, listening, and functional use of English. The **Lab Guide** contains photocopiable pages that guide students through the activities.

The **Teacher-Training Video** offers clear guidance for teaching each section of the Student's Book and professional development activities appropriate for individual or group use.

APPROACH AND METHODOLOGY

New Interchange teaches students to use English for everyday situations and purposes related to school, social life, work, and leisure. The underlying philosophy is that learning a second or foreign language is more rewarding, meaningful, and effective when the language is used for authentic communication. Throughout *New Interchange,* students are presented with natural and useful language. In addition, students have the opportunity to personalize the language they learn, make use of their own knowledge and experiences, and express their ideas and opinions.

KEY FEATURES

Adult and International Content *New Interchange* deals with contemporary topics that are of high interest and relevant to both students and teachers. The topics have been selected for their interest to both homogeneous and heterogeneous classes.

Integrated Syllabus *New Interchange* has an integrated, multi-skills syllabus that links topics, communicative functions, and grammar. Grammar – seen as an essential component of second and foreign language proficiency and competence – is always presented communicatively, with controlled accuracy-based activities leading to fluency-based communicative practice. In this way, there is a link between grammatical form and communicative function. The syllabus is carefully graded, with a gradual progression of teaching items.

Enjoyable and Useful Learning Activities A variety of interesting and enjoyable activities provides thorough individual student practice and enables learners to apply the language they learn. The course also makes extensive use of information-gap tasks; role plays; and pair, group, and whole class activities. Task-based and information-sharing activities provide a maximum amount of student-generated communication.

WHAT EACH UNIT CONTAINS

Snapshot The Snapshots graphically present interesting real-world information that introduces the topic of a unit or cycle, and also develop vocabulary. Follow-up questions encourage discussion of the Snapshot material and personalize the topic.

Conversation The Conversations introduce the new grammar of each cycle in a communicative context and present functional and conversational expressions.

Grammar Focus The new grammar of each unit is presented in color boxes and is followed by controlled and freer communicative practice activities. These freer activities often have students use the grammar in a personal context.

Fluency Exercise These pair, group, whole class, or role-play activities provide more personal practice of the new teaching points and increase the opportunity for individual student practice.

Pronunciation These exercises focus on important features of spoken English, including stress, rhythm, intonation, reductions, and blending.

Listening The Listening activities develop a wide variety of listening skills, including listening for gist, listening for details, and inferring meaning from context. Charts or graphics often accompany these task-based exercises to lend support to students.

Word Power The Word Power activities develop students' vocabulary through a variety of interesting tasks, such as word maps and collocation exercises. Word Power activities are usually followed by oral or written practice that helps students understand how to use the vocabulary in context.

Writing The Writing exercises include practical writing tasks that extend and reinforce the teaching points in the unit and help develop student's compositional skills. The Teacher's Edition demonstrates how to use the models and exercises to focus on the process of writing.

Reading The reading passages use various types of texts adapted from authentic sources. The Readings develop a variety of reading skills, including reading for details, skimming, scanning, and making inferences. Also included are pre-reading and post-reading questions that use the topic of the reading as a springboard to discussion.

Interchange Activities The Interchange Activities are pair work, group work, or whole class activities involving information sharing and role playing to encourage real communication. These exercises are a central part of the course and allow students to extend and personalize what they have practiced and learned in each unit.

Unit Summaries Unit Summaries are located at the back of the Student's Book. They contain lists of the key vocabulary and functional expressions, as well as grammar extensions for each unit.

FROM THE AUTHORS

We hope that you will like using *New Interchange* and find it useful, interesting, and fun. Our goal has been to provide teachers and students with activities that make the English class a time to look forward to and, at the same time, provide students with the skills they need to use English outside the classroom. Please let us know how you enjoy it and good luck!

Jack C. Richards
Jonathan Hull
Susan Proctor

Authors' Acknowledgments

A great number of people contributed to the development of *New Interchange.* Particular thanks are owed to the following:

The **reviewers** using the first edition of *Interchange* in the following schools and institutes – the insights and suggestions of these teachers and their students have helped define the content and format of the new edition: Jorge Haber Resque, **Centro Cultural Brasil-Estados Unidos (CCBEU),** Belém, Brazil; Lynne Roecklein, **Gifu University,** Japan; Mary Oliveira and Montserrat M. Djmal, **Instituto Brasil-Esatdos Unidos (IBEU),** Rio de Janeiro, Brazil; Liliana Baltra, **Instituto Chileno Norte-Americano,** Santiago de Chile; Blanca Arazi and the teachers at **Instituto Cultural Argentino Norteamericano (ICANA),** Buenos Aires, Argentina; Mike Millin and Kelley Seymour, **James English School,** Japan; Matilde Legorreta, **Kratos, S.A. de C.V.,** Mexico D.F.; Peg Donner, Ricia Doren, and Andrew Sachar, **Rancho Santiago College Centennial Education Center,** Santa Ana, California, USA; James Hale, **Sundai ELS,** Japan; Christopher Lynch, **Sunshine College,** Tokyo, Japan; Valerie Benson, **Suzugamine Women's College,** Hiroshima, Japan; Michael Barnes, **Tokyu Be Seminar,** Japan; Claude Arnaud and Paul Chris McVay, **Toyo Women's College,** Tokyo, Japan; Maria Emilia Rey Silva, **UCBEU,** São Paulo, Brazil; Lilia Ortega Sepulveda, **Unidad Lomoa Hermosa,** Mexico D.F.; Eric Bray, **Kyoto YMCA English School,** Kyoto, Japan; John Pak, **Yokohama YMCA English School,** Yokohama, Japan; and the many teachers around the world who responded to the *Interchange* questionnaire.

The **editorial** and **production** team: Suzette André, Sylvia P. Bloch, John Borrelli, Mary Carson, Natalie Nordby Chen, Karen Davy, Randee Falk, Andrew Gitzy, Pauline Ireland, Penny Laporte, Kathy Niemczyk, Kathleen Schultz, Rosie Stamp, and Mary Vaughn.

And Cambridge University Press **staff** and **advisors**: Carlos Barbisan, Kate Cory-Wright, Riitta da Costa, Peter Davison, Peter Donovan, Cecilia Gómez, Colin Hayes, Thares Keeree, Jinsook Kim, Koen Van Landeghem, Carine Mitchell, Sabina Sahni, Helen Sandiford, Dan Schulte, Ian Sutherland, Chris White, and Ellen Zlotnick.

Plan of the Book

Listening/Pronunciation	Writing/Reading	Interchange Activity
		PAGE IC-2 UNIT 1
Recognizing formal and informal names; listening for personal information Intonation of clarification questions	Writing questions requesting personal information "Meeting and Greeting Customs": Reading about greeting customs	"Getting to know you": Collecting personal information from classmates PAGE IC-3 UNIT 2
Listening to descriptions of jobs and daily schedules Unstressed words	Writing a description of an occupation "The Daily Grind": Reading about students with part-time work	"Common ground": Finding similarities in classmates' daily schedules PAGE IC-4 and IC-5 UNIT 3
Listening to people shopping; listening for items, prices, and opinions Linked sounds	Writing a comparison of prices in different countries "Shop Till You Drop": Reading about different kinds of shopping	"Swap meet": Buying and selling things PAGE IC-6 UNIT 4
Identifying musical styles; listening for likes and dislikes; listening to invitations Question intonation	Writing invitations and excuses "The Sound of Music": Reading about musicians from around the world	"What an invitation! What an excuse!": Making up unusual invitations and excuses REVIEW OF UNITS 1–4
		PAGE IC-7 UNIT 5
Listening for family relationships; listening to information about families and family life Blending with *does*	Writing a description of family life "The Changing Family": Reading about an American family	"Family facts": Finding out information about classmates' families and family members PAGE IC-8 UNIT 6
Listening to people talk about free-time activities; listening to routines; listening to descriptions of sports participation Sentence stress	Writing a description of favorite activities "Smart Moves": Reading about fitness for the brain	"Fitness quiz": Interviewing about fitness habits PAGE IC-9 and IC-10 UNIT 7
Listening to descriptions and opinions of past events and vacations Reduced forms of *did you*	Writing a postcard "Vacation Postcards": Reading about different kinds of vacations	"Vacation photos": Telling a story using pictures PAGE IC-11 UNIT 8
Listening for locations of places; listening to descriptions of places in neighborhoods Reduced forms of *there is* and *there are*	Writing a description of a home "City Scenes": Reading about neighborhood life in cities around the world	"Neighborhood survey": Comparing two neighborhoods REVIEW OF UNITS 5–8

Listening/Pronunciation	Writing/Reading	Interchange Activity
		PAGES IC-12 and IC-14 UNIT 9
Listening to descriptions of people; identifying people Contrastive stress	Writing a description of someone "Hip-Hop Fashions": Reading about clothing styles	"Find the differences": Comparing two pictures of a party
		PAGE IC-13 UNIT 10
Listening for time and place of an event; listening to descriptions of events Pronunciation of *have*	Writing a description of an unusual activity "Taking the Risk": Reading about unusual or dangerous sports	"Lifestyles survey": Finding out about a classmate's lifestyle
		PAGE IC-15 UNIT 11
Listening to descriptions of cities and hometowns; listening for incorrect information Pronunciation of *can't* and *shouldn't*	Writing a description of an interesting city "Famous Cities": Reading about cities around the world	"City guide": Creating a city guide
		PAGE IC-16 UNIT 12
Listening to advice; listening to requests in a drugstore Reduced form of *to*	Writing about a home remedy "Grandma Knows Best!": Reading about home remedies	"Talk radio": Giving advice to callers on a radio program
		REVIEW OF UNITS 9-12
		PAGES IC-17 and IC-18 UNIT 13
Listening to people make dinner plans; listening to restaurant orders Stress in responses	Writing a restaurant review "To Tip or Not to Tip?": Reading about tipping customs	"Are you ready to order?": Ordering a meal in a restaurant
		PAGE IC-19 UNIT 14
Listening to a TV game show; listening for information about a country Intonation in questions of choice	Writing about an interesting or beautiful place "Things You Can Do to Help the Environment": Reading about the environment	"How much do you know?": Taking a quiz on general knowledge
		PAGE IC-20 UNIT 15
Listening for information about invitations; receiving telephone messages Reduced forms of *could you* and *would you*	Writing a request to give a message "Ways to Keep Phone Calls Short": Reading about telephone manners	"What are you going to do?": Finding out about classmates' weekend plans
		PAGE IC-21 UNIT 16
Listening to descriptions of changes; listening to hopes for the future Reduced form of *to*	Writing about future plans "The Future Looks Bright": Reading about the plans of three successful students	"Unfold your future!": Planning a possible future
		REVIEW OF UNITS 13-16
		UNIT SUMMARIES
		APPENDIX

1 Please call me Chuck.

1 CONVERSATION *Introducing yourself*

Listen and practice.

Elizabeth: Hello, I'm Elizabeth Mandel.
Chuck: Hi! My name is Charles Chang. But please call me Chuck.
Elizabeth: Nice to meet you, Chuck. You can call me Liz.
Chuck: OK. And what's your last name again?
Elizabeth: Mandel.

2 CHECKING INFORMATION

A Match the questions in column A with the responses in column B. Listen and check. Then practice with a partner. Give your own information.

A

1. How do you pronounce your last name? ....
2. Excuse me, what's your first name again? ....
3. How do you spell your last name? ....
4. What do people call you? ....

B

a. C-H-A-N-G.
b. It's Mandel, with the accent on "del."
c. Well, everyone calls me Chuck.
d. Oh, it's Amy.

B ***Group work*** Make a list of names and nicknames for your group. Introduce yourself with your full name. Use the expressions above.

A: Hi! I'm Joseph Block. Please call me Joe.
B: OK, Joe. And what's your last name again?
A: It's Block.

3 NAMES AND TITLES

A Use a title with a last name to address someone formally.

	Titles	Single	Married
males:	Mr.	✓	✓
females:	Ms.	✓	✓
	Miss	✓	☐
	Mrs.	☐	✓

Use a first name or nickname without a title to address someone informally.

CLASS AUDIO ONLY

B Listen to people talk to Chuck Chang, Elizabeth Mandel, and Amy Kim. Do they address them formally (**F**) or informally (**I**)?

1. .... 2. .... 3. .... 4. .... 5. .... 6. ....

4 CONVERSATION *Introducing someone*

A Listen and practice.

Tom: Paulo, who is that over there?
Paulo: Oh, that's my father! And that's my mother with him.
Tom: I'd like to meet them.

Paulo: Mom and Dad, this is Tom Hayes. Tom, these are my parents.
Tom: Pleased to meet you, Mr. and Mrs. Tavares.
Mrs. Tavares: Nice to meet you, Tom.
Paulo: My parents are here from Brazil. They're on vacation.
Tom: Oh, where are you from in Brazil?
Mr. Tavares: We're from Rio.

B ***Group work*** Take turns introducing a partner to others.

A: Juan, this is Maria. She's from Argentina.
B: Hi, Maria.

5 GRAMMAR FOCUS

Wh-questions and statements with *be*

		Contractions		Subject pronouns	Possessive adjectives
What's your name?	My name **is** Chuck.	I am	= **I'm**	I	my
Where are you from?	**I'm** from Taiwan.	You are	= You**'re**	you	your
Who is that?	His name **is** Tom.	He is	= He**'s**	he	his
What's her name?	Her name **is** Amy.	She is	= She**'s**	she	her
Where is she from?	She**'s** from Korea.	It is	= It**'s**	it	its
Where are you from?	We**'re** from the United States.	We are	= We**'re**	we	our
Who are they?	They**'re** Amy's parents.	They are	= They**'re**	you	your
What are their names?	Their names **are** Mr. and Mrs. Kim.	What is	= What**'s**	they	their
Where are they from?	They**'re** from Korea.				

For a list of countries and nationalities, see the appendix at the back of the book.

A Complete this conversation. Then compare with a partner.

Yoko: Rich, who are the two women over there?
Rich: Oh, ... names are Lisa and Kate.

Rich: Hi, Kate. This .... Yoko. .... from Japan.
Yoko: Hello. Nice to meet you.
Kate: Good to meet you, Yoko.
Lisa: And .... name .... Lisa.
Yoko: Hi, Lisa.
Rich: Lisa and Kate .... from Canada.
Yoko: Oh? Where .... you from in Canada?
Kate: .... from Toronto.

B Complete these questions. Then practice with a partner.

1. A: *Who* .... *is* .... that?
   B: That's Rich.
2. A: .... he from?
   B: He's from Los Angeles.
3. A: .... his last name?
   B: It's Brown.
4. A: .... the two students over there?
   B: Their names are Lisa and Kate.
5. A: .... they from?
   B: They're from Canada.

C ***Group work*** Write five questions about your classmates. Then take turns asking and answering your questions.

Who is she?
Where is Su Hee from?

6 SNAPSHOT

Source: Brigham Young University, Center for International Studies

Talk about these questions.

Which greetings are typical in your country?
Can you name a country for each greeting?

7 CONVERSATION *Asking about someone*

A Listen and practice.

Sarah: Hi, Tom. How's everything?
Tom: Not bad. How are you?
Sarah: Pretty good, thanks.

Tom: Sarah, this is Paulo. He's from Brazil.
Sarah: Hello, Paulo. Are you on vacation?
Paulo: No, I'm not. I'm a student here.
Sarah: Oh, are you studying English?
Paulo: Well, yes, I am. And engineering, too.
Sarah: Are you and Tom in the same class?
Paulo: No, we aren't. But we're on the same volleyball team.

CLASS AUDIO ONLY

B Listen to the rest of the conversation.

Where is Sarah from?

8 GRAMMAR FOCUS

Yes/No questions and short answers with be

Are you on vacation? — No, **I'm not**. **I'm** a student.
Are you a student? — Yes, I **am**.

Is Sarah from the United States? — No, she **isn't**. (No, she**'s not**.) She**'s** from Australia.
Is Sarah from Australia? — Yes, she **is**.

Are you and Tom in the same class? — No, we **aren't**. (No, we**'re not**.) We**'re** on the same volleyball team.
Are you and Tom on the volleyball team? — Yes, we **are**.

Are Mr. and Mrs. Tavares American? — No, they **aren't**. (No, they**'re not**.) They**'re** Brazilian.
Are Mr. and Mrs. Tavares Brazilian? — Yes, they **are**.

A Complete these conversations. Then practice with a partner.

1. A: .... you from the United States?
   B: Yes, I .... from Chicago.
2. A: .... Rosa in English 101?
   B: No, she .... in English 102.
3. A: .... you and Monique from France?
   B: Yes, we .... from Paris.

B ***Pair work*** Read the conversations in Exercises 4 and 7 again. Then answer these questions. For questions you answer "no," give the correct information.

1. Are Tom and Paulo on the baseball team? ....
2. Are Mr. and Mrs. Tavares on vacation? ....
3. Are Mr. and Mrs. Tavares from Mexico? ....
4. Is Paulo from Brazil? ....
5. Is Paulo on vacation? ....

C ***Group work*** Write five questions about your classmates. Then take turns asking and answering your questions.

Are Maria and Su Hee friends?

interchange 1
Getting to know you
Find out about your classmates. Turn to page IC-2.

9 LISTENING

CLASS AUDIO ONLY

Listen to these conversations and complete the information about each person.

First name	Last name	Where from?	Studying?
1. *Joe*	....	*the United States*	....
2.	*Vera*	....	*engineering*
3. *Min Ho*	*Kim*	....	....

10 READING

Meeting and Greeting Customs

How do you think the people in these countries greet each other?

There are many different greeting customs around the world. Here are some.

Chile

People usually shake hands when they meet for the first time. When two women first meet, they sometimes give one kiss on the cheek. (They actually "kiss the air.") Women also greet both male and female friends with a kiss. Chilean men give their friends warm *abrazos* (hugs) or sometimes kiss women on the cheek.

Finland

Finns greet each other with a firm handshake. Hugs and kisses are only for close friends and family.

The Philippines

The everyday greeting for friends is a handshake for both men and women. Men sometimes pat each other on the back.

Korea

Men bow slightly and shake hands to greet each other. Women do not usually shake hands. To address someone with his or her full name, the family name comes first, then the first name.

The United States

People shake hands when they are first introduced. Friends and family members often hug or kiss on the cheek when they see each other. In these situations, men often kiss women but not other men.

A According to the article, in which country or countries are the following true? Check (✓) the correct boxes.

	Chile	Finland	the Philippines	Korea	the U.S.
1. People shake hands every time they meet.	☐	☐	☐	☐	☐
2. Women do not shake hands.	☐	☐	☐	☐	☐
3. Women kiss at the first meeting.	☐	☐	☐	☐	☐
4. Men hug or pat each other on the back.	☐	☐	☐	☐	☐
5. Women kiss male friends.	☐	☐	☐	☐	☐
6. The family name comes first.	☐	☐	☐	☐	☐

B ***Pair work*** How do these people greet each other in your country?

1. two male friends
2. a male and female friend
3. two strangers
4. two female friends

2 How do you spend your day?

1 SNAPSHOT

Work and School Days

	Brazil	the United Kingdom	South Korea	the United States
Average number of working hours per week	44	44	48	40
Average number of paid vacation days per year	20–21	27	20	12
Number of national holidays	10	8	10	11
Number of school days per year	182	192	222	178
Hours of instruction in school per day	4.5	5	4.5	5.5

Information compiled from *The New York Times, Digest of Educational Statistics,* and interviews.

Talk about these questions.

Which country would you like to work in? Why?
Where would you like to be a student? Why?

2 WORD POWER *Jobs*

A Complete the word map with jobs from the list.

architect
receptionist
company director
flight attendant
supervisor
engineer
salesperson
secretary
professor
sales manager
security guard
word processor

Jobs

Professionals
architect ....
....
....
....
....

Service occupations
flight attendant ....
....
....
....
....

Management positions
company director ....
....
....
....
....

Office work
receptionist ....
....
....
....
....

B Add two more jobs to each category. Then compare with a partner.

3 WORK AND WORKPLACES

A Look at the pictures. Match the information in columns A, B, and C.

A	*B*	*C*
a salesperson	for an airline	builds houses
a chef	in a restaurant	cares for patients
a flight attendant	for a construction company	answers the phone
a carpenter	in a hospital	cooks food
a receptionist	in a department store	serves passengers
a nurse	in an office	sells clothes

B ***Pair work*** Take turns describing each person's job.

"She's a salesperson. She works in a department store. She sells clothes."

4 CONVERSATION *Describing work*

A Listen and practice.

Jason: Where do you work, Andrea?
Andrea: I work for Thomas Cook Travel.
Jason: Oh, really? What do you do there?
Andrea: I'm a guide. I take people on tours to countries in South America, like Peru.
Jason: That sounds interesting!
Andrea: Yes, it's a great job. I love it. And what do you do?
Jason: I'm a student, and I have a part-time job, too.
Andrea: Oh? Where do you work?
Jason: In a fast-food restaurant.
Andrea: Which restaurant?
Jason: Hamburger Heaven.

CLASS AUDIO ONLY

B Listen to the rest of the conversation.

1. What does Jason do, exactly?
2. How does he like his job?

5 GRAMMAR FOCUS

Simple present Wh-questions and statements

		I/You	He/She
What do you **do**?	**I'm** a student, and I **have** a part-time job.	work	works
Where do you **work**?	I **work** at/in a restaurant.	take	takes
Where do you **go** to school?	I **go** to the University of Texas.	study	studies
How do you **like** your school?	I **like** it very much.	teach	teaches
Where does Andrea **work**?	She **works** for Thomas Cook Travel.	do	does
What does she **do**?	She's a guide. She **takes** people on tours.	go	goes
Where does Jason **go** to school?	He **goes** to New York University.	have	has
How does he **like** it?	He **loves** it.		

A Complete these conversations. Then practice with a partner.

1. A: What do you do ?
   B: I'm a student. I study business.
   A: And where do you go to school?
   B: I go to Jefferson College.
   A: How do you like your classes?
   B: I like them a lot.

2. A: What does Kanya do?
   B: She's a teacher. She teaches mathematics at a school in Bangkok.
   A: And what about Somsak? Where does he work?
   B: He works for an electronics company.
   A: What does he do, exactly?
   B: He's a salesman. He sells computer equipment.

B *Pair work* What do you know about these jobs? Complete the chart. Then write sentences describing each job, using *he* or *she*.

A doctor	A travel agent	A police officer
▪ *works in a hospital*	▪	▪ ....
▪ *has an office*	▪	▪ ....
▪ *works long hours*	▪	▪ ....
▪ *cares for patients*	▪	▪ ....

A doctor works in a hospital. She has an office, too. . . .

C *Group work* Ask your classmates questions about work and school.

A: What do you do, Aki?
B: I'm a student.
C: Where do you go to school?
B: . . .

6 WRITING

A Write a description of what you do. Don't write your name on the paper.

I'm a student. I go to McGill University in Canada. I'm a freshman. I study computer science. I work part time at a radio station, too. I'm a disc jockey. I play music. I love my job!

B ***Group work*** Pass your descriptions around the group. Can you guess who wrote each description?

7 CONVERSATION *Daily schedules*

A Listen and practice.

Daniel: How do you spend your day, Helen?
Helen: Well, on weekdays I get up around ten. Then I read the paper for an hour and have lunch at about noon.
Daniel: Really? What time do you go to work?
Helen: I start work at three.
Daniel: And when do you get home at night?
Helen: I get home pretty late, around midnight.
Daniel: So what do you do, exactly?
Helen: I'm a TV announcer. Don't you recognize me? I do the weather report on KNTV!
Daniel: Gee, I'm sorry. I don't watch TV.

CLASS AUDIO ONLY

B Listen to Daniel describe how he spends his day.

1. What time does he get up? start work? study until?
2. What does he do?

8 PRONUNCIATION *Unstressed words*

A Listen and practice. The prepositions in these sentences (*around, for,* and *at*) are not stressed.

I get **úp** around **tén.**
I read the **páper** for an **hóur**.
I have **lúnch** at about **nóon**.

B ***Pair work*** Practice the conversation in Exercise 7 again. Be careful not to stress prepositions.

9 GRAMMAR FOCUS

Time expressions

I get up	**at** 7:00	**in** the morning	**on** weekdays.
I go to bed	**around** ten	**in** the evening	**on** weeknights.
I leave work	**early**	**in** the afternoon	**on** weekends.
I get home	**late**	**at** night	**on** Fridays.
I stay up	**until** midnight	**on** Saturdays.	
I wake up	**before/after** noon	**on** Sundays.	

Ways to express clock time
7:00
seven o'clock
seven
7:00 in the morning = 7:00 A.M.
7:00 in the evening = 7:00 P.M.

A Complete these sentences with time expressions.

1. I get up around/at six in the morning on weekdays.
2. I go to bed at midnight on weeknights.
3. I start work at 11:30 at night.
4. I arrive at work early on Mondays, at 7:00 A.M.
5. I have lunch at three in the afternoon on weekdays.
6. I stay up late on weekends.
7. I have a little snack around 9:00 in the evening.
8. I sleep until noon on Sundays.

B Rewrite the sentences above so that they are true for you. Then compare with a partner.

C ***Pair work*** Take turns asking and answering these questions.

1. What days do you get up early? late?
2. What are two things you do before 8:00 in the morning?
3. What are three things you do on Saturday mornings?
4. How late do you stay up on Saturday nights?
5. What is something you do only on Sundays?

interchange 2

Common ground

Take a survey. Compare your schedule with your classmates' schedules. Turn to page IC-3.

10 LISTENING

CLASS AUDIO ONLY

A Listen to Rodney, Tina, and Ellen talk about their daily schedules. Complete the chart.

	Job	Gets up at . . .	Gets home at . . .	Goes to bed at . . .
Rodney				
Tina				
Ellen				

B ***Class activity*** Who do you think has the best daily schedule? Why?

11 READING

The Daily Grind

Is it a good idea for a student to have a job? Why or why not?

Brandon Smith

I'm a junior in high school, and I have a part-time job in a restaurant. I bus dishes on Saturdays and Sundays from 8:00 until 4:00. I earn $5.50 an hour. It isn't much money, but I save almost every penny! I want to go to a good university, and the cost goes up every year. Of course, I spend some money when I go out on Saturday nights.

Lauren Russell

I'm a senior in high school. I have a job as a cashier in a grocery store. The job pays well – about $6.75 an hour. I work every weeknight after school from 4:00 until 8:00. I don't have time for homework, and my grades aren't very good this year. But I have to work, or I can't buy nice clothes and I can't go out on Saturday nights. Also, a car costs a lot of money.

Erica Davis

I'm a freshman in college. College is very expensive, so I work in a law office for three hours every weekday afternoon. I make photocopies, file papers, and sort mail for $8.25 an hour. The job gives me good experience because I want to be a lawyer someday. But I don't want to work every semester. I need time to study.

A Read the article. Why do these students work? Check (✓) the correct boxes.

	Brandon	Lauren	Erica
1. To earn money for college	☐	☐	☐
2. To buy nice clothes	☐	☐	☐
3. To go out on the weekend	☐	☐	☐
4. To pay for a car	☐	☐	☐
5. To get job experience	☐	☐	☐

B ***Pair work*** Talk about these questions.

1. Look at the reasons why each student works. Who has good reasons to work? Who doesn't, in your opinion?
2. How many hours a week does each student work?
3. How much money does each student earn per week?
4. What are the advantages and disadvantages of part-time work for students?

3 How much is it?

1 SNAPSHOT

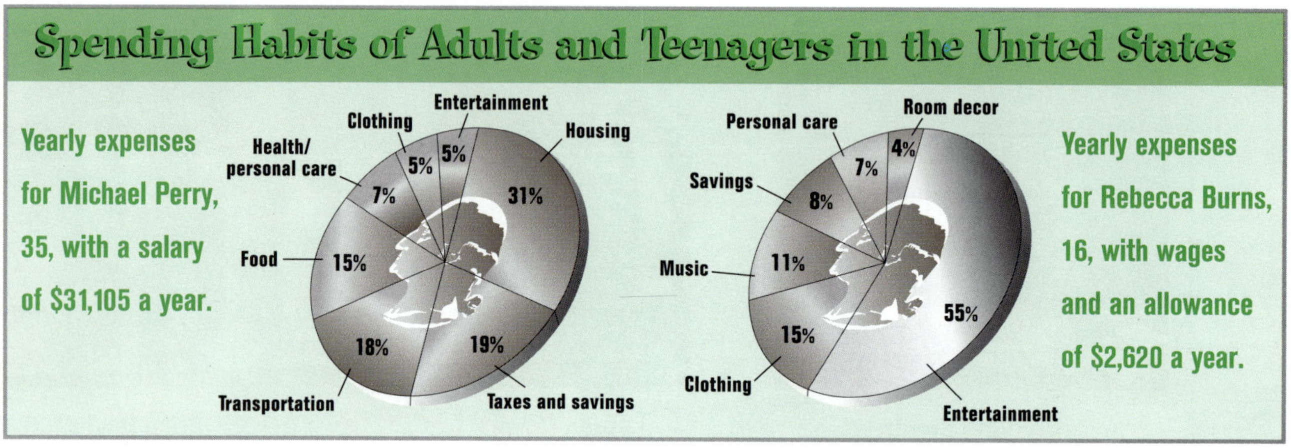

Portraits based on information from the *Statistical Abstract of the U.S.* and the Rand Youth Poll.

Talk about these questions.

How does Michael Perry spend most of his money?
How does Rebecca Burns spend most of her money?
How do their spending habits compare?
How do you spend your money? Make two lists: things you have to buy and things you like to buy.

2 CONVERSATION *Prices*

A Listen and practice.

Steve: Oh, look at those earrings, Maria. They're perfect for you.
Maria: These red ones? I'm not sure.
Steve: No, the yellow ones.
Maria: Oh, these? Hmm. Yellow isn't a good color for me.
Steve: Well, that necklace isn't bad.
Maria: Which one?
Steve: That blue one right there. How much is it?
Maria: It's $42! That's expensive!
Steve: Hey, let me get it for you. It's your birthday present.

CLASS AUDIO ONLY

B Listen to the rest of the conversation.

1. What else do they buy?
2. Who pays for it?

3 GRAMMAR FOCUS

Demonstratives; one, ones

How much is **this** necklace? **this one**? How much are **these** earrings? **these**?	How much is **that** necklace? **that one**? How much are **those** earrings? **those**?	Which **one**? The blue **one**. It's $42. Which **ones**? The yellow **ones**. They're $18.

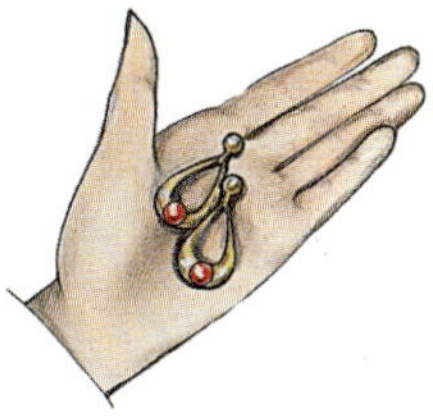

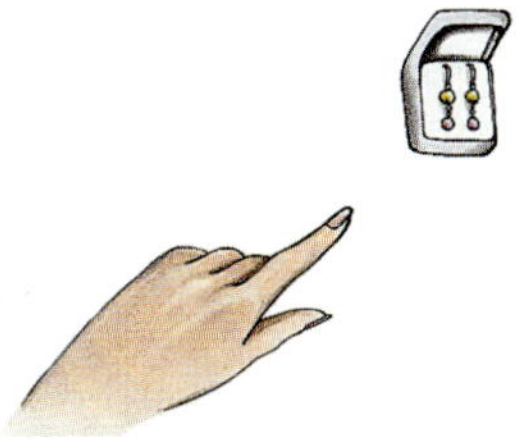

Prices
$42 = forty-two dollars
$59.95 = fifty-nine ninety-five
or fifty-nine dollars and ninety-five cents

Colors

light blue	dark blue	green	yellow
orange	pink	red	purple
brown	black	gray	white

Look at the pictures and complete these conversations.
Then practice with a partner.

1. A: Excuse me. How much .... jeans?
   B: Which .... ? Do you mean .... ?
   A: No, the light blue ....
   B: Oh, ... $59.95.
   A: Almost sixty dollars! Are you kidding?

2. A: I like .... backpack over there. How much .... it?
   B: Which .... ? Each backpack has a different price.
   A: .... red ....
   B: It's $98.50. But .... green .... is only $45.
   A: OK. Let me look at it.

4 THAT'S EXPENSIVE!

Pair work Ask and answer questions about these products. For help with numbers, see the appendix at the back of the book.

A: How much is the computer?
B: Which one?
A: The small one./This one.
B: It's $5,456.
A: That's expensive!

useful expressions

That's cheap.
That's reasonable.
That's OK/not bad.
That's expensive.

5 LISTENING

CLASS AUDIO ONLY

Listen to Tim and Sandra shopping, and complete the chart.

Item	Price	Do they buy it? Yes	No	Reason
1. Rollerblades	....	☐	☐	....
2. cap	....	☐	☐	....
3. sunglasses	....	☐	☐	....

6 PRONUNCIATION *Linked sounds*

A Listen and practice. Final consonants are often linked to the vowels that follow them.

A: How much are these pants?
B: They're forty-eight dollars.

A: And how much is this sweater?
B: It's thirty-seven dollars.

B ***Pair work*** Ask and answer four questions about prices in this unit. Pay attention to the linked sounds.

interchange 3

Swap meet

See what kinds of deals you can make as a buyer and a seller. Turn to pages IC-4 and IC-5.

7 WORD POWER *Materials*

A ***Pair work*** Identify these things. Use the words from the list.
What other materials are these things sometimes made of? Make a list.

a **cotton** shirt	**leather** gloves	a **plastic** bracelet	a **silk** scarf
a **gold** ring	**polyester** pants	**rubber** boots	**silver** earrings

1. gold ring 2. plastic bracelet 3. silk scarf 4. polyester pants

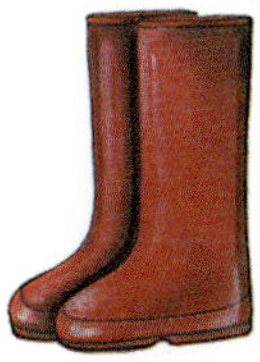

5. leather gloves 6. cotton shirt 7. silver earrings 8. rubber boots

B ***Class activity*** Which of the materials can you find in your classroom?

"Juan has a leather bag."

8 CONVERSATION *Shopping*

A Listen and practice.

Anne: Look! These jackets are nice. Which one do you like better?
Sue: I like the wool one better.
Anne: Really? Why?
Sue: It looks warmer.
Anne: Well, I prefer the leather one. It's more attractive than the wool one.
Sue: Hmm. There's no price tag.
Anne: Excuse me. How much is this jacket?
Clerk: It's $499. Would you like to try it on?
Anne: Oh, no. That's OK! But thank you anyway.
Clerk: You're welcome.

CLASS AUDIO ONLY

B Listen to the rest of the conversation.

1. What does Anne buy?
2. What does Sue think of it?

9 GRAMMAR FOCUS

Comparisons

Preferences; comparisons with adjectives

Which one do you **prefer?** I **prefer** the leather one. Which one do you **like better/more?** I **like** the leather one **better/more.**	That one is **nicer than** the wool one. This one is **cheaper than** . . . . The leather jacket is **prettier than** . . . . It looks **bigger than** . . . . It's **more attractive than**	nice → nic**er** cheap → cheap**er** pretty → prett**ier** big → big**ger** good → **better**

For more information on comparatives, see the appendix at the back of the book.

A Complete these conversations. Then practice with a partner.

polyester tie   silk tie   medium shirt   large shirt   leather boots   rubber boots

1. A: Which tie is ...prettier..., the orange one or the blue one? (pretty)
   B: Well, the blue one is silk. And silk is ...nicer than the... polyester. (nice)

2. A: Is this green shirt ...larger than... that yellow one? (large)
   B: No, the yellow one is ~~larger~~ .... It's a large. The green one is a medium. (big)

3. A: Which are ...Cheaper..., the brown boots or the black ones? (cheap)
   B: The brown ones are leather. And leather is ...more... rubber. (expensive)

B ***Pair work*** Compare the items above with a partner. Give your own opinions.

A: Which tie do you like better?
B: I like the orange one better. The design is nicer.

useful expressions

The color is prettier.
The design is nicer.
The style is more attractive.
The material is better.

10 WRITING

How much do these items cost in your country? Fill in the chart. Then compare the prices in your country with the prices in the U.S.

	Cost in my country	Cost in the U.S.
gasoline	....	$ 1.10/gallon
a compact disc	....	$ 12.99
a haircut	....	$ 23.00
a pair of jeans	....	$ 34.00

Many things are more expensive in my country than in the United States. For example, a liter of gas is about $.66. In the U.S. it's cheaper. It's about $1.10 per gallon. . . .

11 READING

Shop Till You Drop

Look at the pictures of different kinds of shopping in the United States. What kind of shopping can you do in your country?

Catalog Shopping

People in the United States often shop from catalogs. There are special catalogs for almost every need – including clothing, furniture, health and beauty products, and things for the kitchen. People also order about 40% of their music from music club catalogs. Customers say that music stores are too noisy.

Television Shopping

Television shopping began in 1986. About 5% to 8% of the American public now shops by television. Some popular shopping channels are the Home Shopping Network and QVC. Customers say that television shopping is easier than shopping in a store. How do they buy things? They make a phone call and charge the item to their credit card. And TV shopping channels are on late at night, so people can "go shopping" anytime.

Computer Shopping

Is computer shopping the way of the future? About 37% of American households now have personal computers. And shopping by computer (or "shopping on-line") is interesting to more people every day. Already, shoppers can use their computers to order many different products, such as computer products, flowers, food, T-shirts, and posters. And new on-line shopping services appear every day. Soon people may be able to shop for anything, anytime, anywhere in the world.

A Read the article. Check (✓) True or False. For the false statements, give the correct information.

	True	False
1. About 60% of music in the United States is sold through music stores.	☐	☐
2. The Home Shopping Network is the name of a computer shopping service.	☐	☐
3. About 37% of American households do their shopping through the computer.	☐	☐

B ***Pair work*** Talk about these questions.

1. Do you like shopping? How often do you usually shop?
2. What kinds of shopping do you like? Check (✓) the appropriate boxes.

☐ shopping at discount stores
☐ television shopping
☐ shopping at department stores
☐ shopping at small stores
☐ catalog shopping
☐ shopping at secondhand or thrift stores
☐ computer shopping
☐ shopping at a mall

4 Do you like jazz?

1 SNAPSHOT

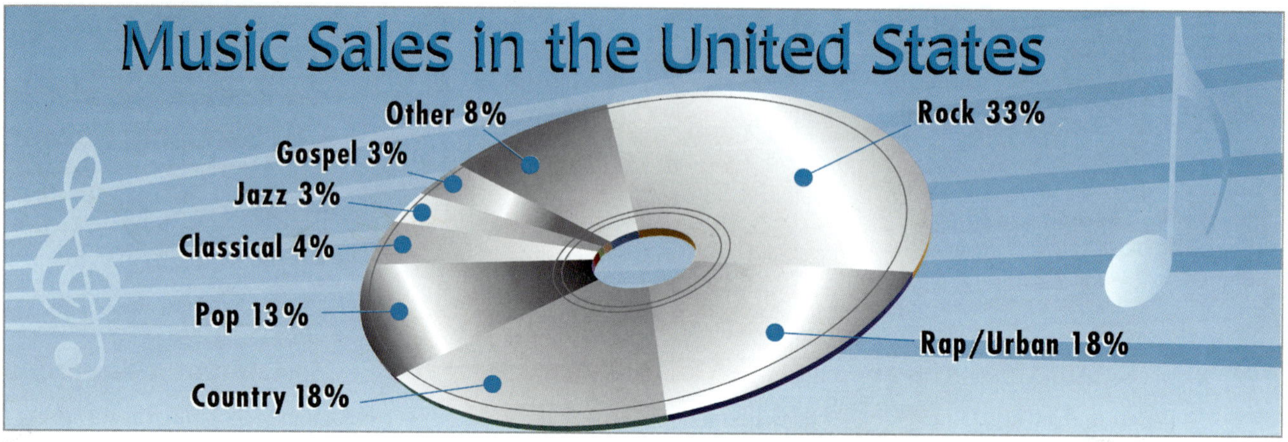

Source: The Recording Industry Association of America

Talk about these questions.

Which of these kinds of music do people in your country listen to?
What other kinds of music do people in your country like?

CLASS AUDIO ONLY

Listen and number the musical styles from 1 to 8 as you hear them.

.... *classical*	.... *gospel*	.... *New Age*	.... *rap*
.... *country*	.... *jazz*	.... *pop*	.... *rock*

2 WORD POWER *Entertainment*

A Complete the chart with words from the list.

classical	salsa
game shows	science fiction
horror films	soap operas
jazz	talk shows
news	thrillers
pop	westerns

B Add three more words to each category. Then compare with a partner.

C Number the items in each list from 1 (you like it the most) to 7 (you like it the least).

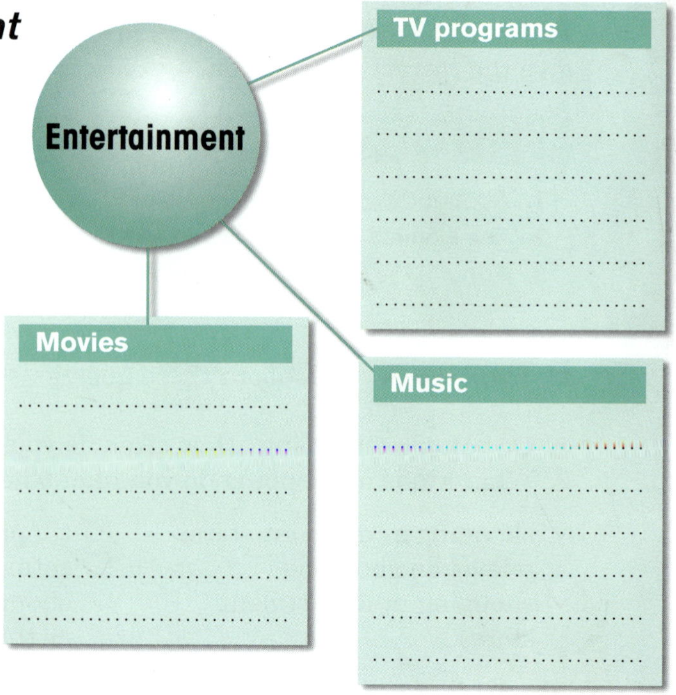

3 CONVERSATION *Likes and dislikes*

A Listen and practice.

Liz: Do you like jazz, Tom?
Tom: No, I don't like it very much. Do you?
Liz: Well, yes, I do. I'm a real fan of Wynton Marsalis.
Tom: Oh, does he play the piano?
Liz: No, he doesn't! He plays the trumpet. So, what kind of music do you like?
Tom: I like rock a lot.
Liz: Who's your favorite group?
Tom: The Cranberries. I love their music. How about you? Do you like them?
Liz: No, I don't. I can't stand them!

CLASS AUDIO ONLY

B Listen to the rest of the conversation.

1. Who is Liz's favorite singer?
2. Does Tom like that singer? Why or why not?

4 GRAMMAR FOCUS

Yes/No and Wh-questions with do

		Object pronouns
Do you **like** jazz? Yes, I **do**. I like it a lot. No, I **don't** like it very much.	**What kind of** music **do** you **like**? I like rock a lot.	me you (singular) him her
Does he **play** the piano? Yes, he **does**. No, he **doesn't**.	**What does** he **play**? He plays the trumpet.	it us
Do they **like** The Cranberries? Yes, they **do**. They love them. No, they **don't** like them very much.	**Who do** they **like**? They like R.E.M.	you (plural) them

Complete these conversations. Then practice with a partner.

1. A: .... you like horror films?
   B: No, I .... like .... very much. I like comedies.
   A: How about Lisa and Brian? .... they like horror films?
   B: Well, I think Brian .... Why don't you ask ....?

2. A: .... you like the singer Bonnie Raitt?
   B: Yes, I .... I really like .... a lot.
   A: What .... of music .... she sing?
   B: She's a rock singer.
   A: .... she sing country music, too?
   B: I don't know. I have her new CD. Let's listen to ....

5 PRONUNCIATION *Question intonation*

A Listen and practice. Yes/No questions usually have rising intonation. Wh-questions usually have falling intonation.

Do you like movies? What kind of movies do you like?

Do you like pop music? What kind of music do you like?

B Practice these questions.

Do you like TV? What programs do you like?
Do you like music videos? What videos do you like?

6 ENTERTAINMENT SURVEY

A *Group work* Write five questions about entertainment and entertainers. Then ask and answer your questions in groups.

Do you like . . . ?
(pop music, TV, movies, plays)
What kinds of . . . do you like?
(music, movies, TV programs)
What do you think of . . . ?
(*Star Trek*, horror films, gospel music)

B *Group work* Complete this information about your group.

Our Group Favorites	
What's your favorite kind of . . . ?	**Who's your favorite . . . ?**
music:	singer: ....
movie:	actor: ....
TV program:	actress: ....

C *Class activity* Read your group's list to the class. Then find out the class favorites.

useful expressions

Our favorite . . . is . . . .
We all like . . . .
We don't agree on . . . .
We can't stand . . . .

7 LISTENING *TV game show*

CLASS AUDIO ONLY

A Listen to four people playing *Who's My Date?* Three men want to invite Linda on a date. What kinds of things do they like? What kinds of things does Linda like?

	Music	Movies	TV programs
Bill	*classical*		
John			
Tony			
Linda			

B ***Class activity*** Who do you think is the best date for Linda?

8 CONVERSATION *Invitations*

Listen and practice.

Dave: I have tickets to *The Phantom of the Opera* on Friday night. Would you like to go?
Susan: Thanks. I'd love to. What time is the show?
Dave: It's at 8:00.
Susan: That sounds great. So, do you want to have dinner at 6:00?
Dave: Uh, I'd like to, but I have to work late.
Susan: Oh, that's OK. Let's just meet at the theater before the show, around 7:30.
Dave: That sounds fine.

a scene from *The Phantom of the Opera*

9 GRAMMAR FOCUS

Would; *verb* + to + *verb*

Would you **like to go** out on Saturday night? Yes, I **would**. Yes, I**'d love to**. Thanks. Yes, I**'d** really **like to go**.	**Would** you **like to see** a movie? **I'd like to**, but I **have to work** late. **I'd like to**, but I **need to save** money. **I'd like to**, but I **want to visit** my parents.	*Contraction* I would = **I'd**

A Respond to these invitations. Then practice with a partner.

1. A: I have tickets to the baseball game on Saturday. Would you like to go?
   B: ....
2. A: Would you like to come over for dinner tonight?
   B: ....
3. A: Would you like to go to the gym with me on Friday night?
   B: ....
4. A: There's a great movie on TV tonight. Would you like to watch it with me?
   B: ....

B ***Pair work*** Think of three different things you would like to do. Then invite a partner to do them with you. Ask and answer follow-up questions like these:

When is it? What time does it start?
Where is it? What time should I/we . . . ?

10 LISTENING

CLASS AUDIO ONLY

Listen to three people inviting friends to events and activities. Complete the chart. Do the friends accept the invitations?

	Event/Activity	Day	Time	Accept? Yes	Accept? No
1. Jake and Paula	....	....	....	☐	☐
2. Lucy and Chris	....	....	....	☐	☐
3. Rich and Ed	....	....	....	☐	☐

11 WRITING

See Interchange 4 for the writing assignment.

interchange 4

What an invitation! What an excuse!

Make up unusual invitations and funny excuses. Turn to page IC-6.

12 READING

The Sound of Music

What are some traditional kinds of music in your country?

Do you like popular music from Latin America, the United States, or Asia? Many musicians from around the world blend their country's music with popular sounds.

Bonnie Raitt

Bonnie Raitt is an American singer, songwriter, and guitarist. Her music blends rock with country and the blues. The blues is a kind of folk music that is often sad. It is usually about love and the problems of life. Bonnie Raitt's strong, rough voice is perfect for singing country and the blues.

Caetano Veloso

After thirty years, Caetano Veloso is still one of Brazil's most important musicians. He mixes rock with the music of the Bahia region. Bahia is a state of Brazil that is strongly influenced by African culture. Caetano Veloso is an excellent songwriter and poet. He says of his music, "I make my records like a painter paints his canvas."

Cui Jian

Cui Jian [pronounced "tsay jyan"] is a very important musician in the growth of rock music in China. Western styles, like jazz and rap, clearly influence his music. However, his music is very Chinese in its instruments and sounds. Cui Jian says his music expresses the feelings of Chinese young people.

A Read about the three musicians. Complete the chart.

	Nationality	Types of music he/she blends
1. Caetano Veloso	....	....
2. Bonnie Raitt	....	....
3. Cui Jian	....	....

B ***Pair work*** Talk about these questions.

1. What do these three musicians have in common?
2. How does Caetano Veloso make his records?
3. Why is Bonnie Raitt's voice good for country and blues music?
4. What does Cui Jian want his music to express?

Review of Units 1–4

1 GETTING TO KNOW YOU

Pair work You are talking to someone at school. Have a conversation.

A: Hi. How are you?
B: . . .
A: By the way, my name is . . . .
B: How do you pronounce your name again?
A: . . . Where are you from?
B: . . .
A: Are you a student here?
B: . . . And how about you? What do you do?
A: . . .
B: Oh, really? And where are you from?
A: . . .
B: Well, nice talking to you. . . .

2 WHAT'S THE QUESTION?

Look at these answers. Write the questions. Then compare with a partner.

1. No, Teresa and I aren't in the same class. She's in the morning class.
2. My sister? She goes to the University of Toronto.
3. I get up before 11:00 A.M. on Sundays.
4. No, my teacher isn't American. She's Canadian.
5. Rock music is OK, but I like jazz better.
6. I leave home at 6:30 in the evening on weekdays.
7. A video? Sure, I'd love to watch one with you.
8. The red sweater is nicer than the purple one.

3 ROLE PLAY *In a department store*

Pair work Put items "for sale" on your desk or a table – notebooks, watches, or bags. Use items of different colors.

Student A: You are a clerk. Answer the customer's questions.

Student B: You are a customer. Ask about the price of each item. Say if you want to buy it.

A: Can I help you?
B: Yes. I like that . . . . How much . . . ?
A: Which one(s)?
B: . . .

Where did you get.

Change roles and try the role play again.

4 LISTENING

CLASS AUDIO ONLY

Listen to people asking questions at a party. Check (✓) the best response.

#29

1. ☐ I work in an office.
   ☑ Yes, very early. Before 7:00 A.M.
2. ☐ Not very much.
   ☑ Oh, I just stay in and work around the house.
3. ☐ Yes, I have a laptop.
   ☑ A good laptop computer costs over $2,000.
4. ☐ Yes, I'm from Italy.
   ☑ Actually, I work here.
5. ☑ Almost any kind except classical.
   ☐ No, I don't play the piano.
6. ☑ Thanks, I'd love to. What time?
   ☐ It's on at the Varsity Theater.

5 TV AND RADIO

A Pair work Take turns asking and answering these questions.

TV

When do you usually watch TV?
What kinds of programs do you prefer?
What's your favorite channel?
What's your favorite program?
What time is it on?
Do you watch . . . (name of program)?

B Pair work Change partners. Take turns asking and answering these questions.

Radio

When do you listen to the radio?
What kinds of programs do you listen to?
Do you listen to programs in English?
What's your favorite radio station?
Who are your favorite singers and groups?
What's your favorite radio program?

5 Tell me about your family.

1 WORD POWER *The family*

A Look at Sam's family tree. How are these people related to him? Add these words to the family tree.

cousin
father
grandmother
niece
sister-in-law
uncle
wife

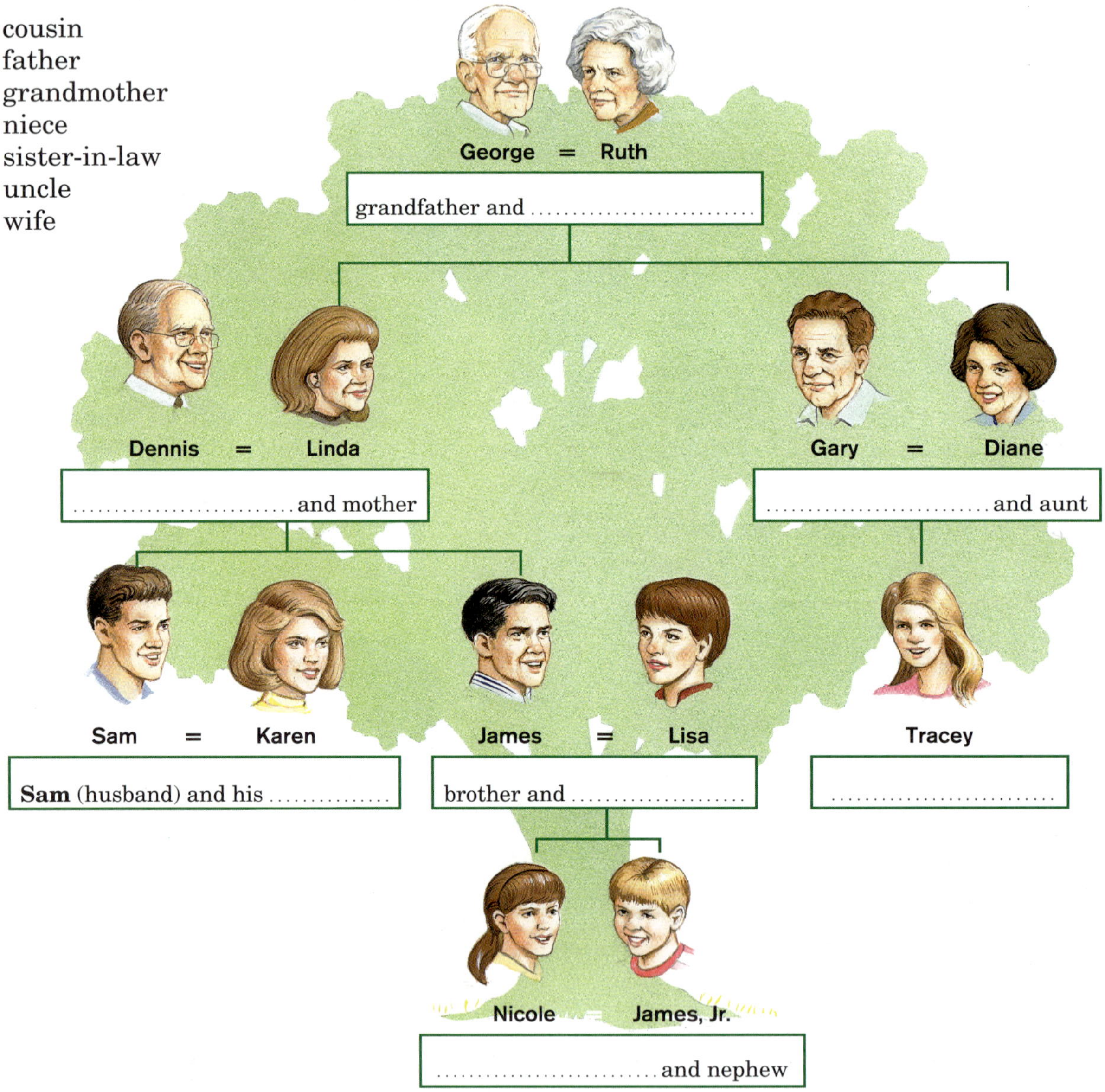

B ***Pair work*** Draw your family tree. Then take turns talking about your families. Ask follow-up questions to get more information.

For a single person:
There are 6 in my family.
I have 2 sisters and a brother.

For a married person:
There are 4 in my family.
We have a daughter and a son.

Follow-up questions:
Where do/does your . . . live?
What do/does your . . . do?

2 LISTENING *Hollywood families*

CLASS AUDIO ONLY

Listen to two conversations about famous people. How are the people related?

1.

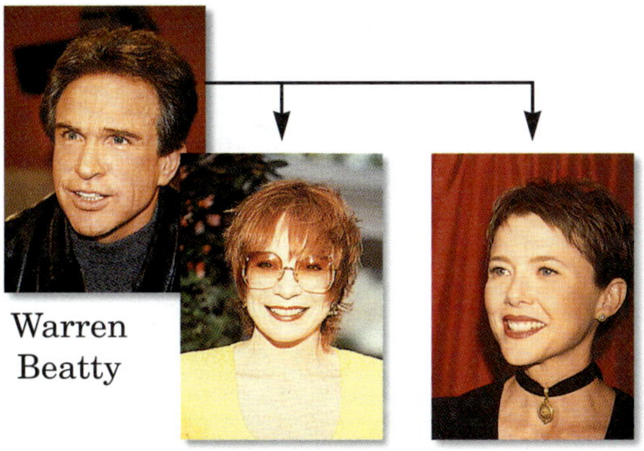

Warren Beatty

Shirley MacLaine ....

Annette Bening ....

2.

Charlie Sheen

Martin Sheen ....

Emilio Estevez ....

3 CONVERSATION *Asking about families*

A Listen and practice.

Rita: Tell me about your brother and sister, Sue.
Sue: Well, my sister is a lawyer.
Rita: Really? Does she live here in Seattle?
Sue: Yes, she does. But she's working in Washington, D.C., right now. Her job is top secret.
Rita: Wow! And what does your brother do?
Sue: He's a painter. He's working in Argentina this month. He has an exhibition there.
Rita: What an interesting family!

CLASS AUDIO ONLY

B Listen to the rest of the conversation.

1. Where do Rita's parents live?
2. What do they do?

4 PRONUNCIATION *Blending with* does

Listen and practice. Notice the blending of **does** with other words.

1. A: My brother is married.
   B: **Does he** [dəziy] have any children?
   A: Yes, he does.
   B: **What does he** [wədəziy] do?
   A: He's a painter.

2. A: My sister lives in Seattle.
   B: **Does she** [dəʃiy] live with you?
   A: No, she doesn't.
   B: **What does she** [wədəʃiy] do?
   A: She's a lawyer.

5 GRAMMAR FOCUS

Present continuous

Are you **living** at home now? **Is** she still **working** in Seattle? **Are** they **going** to college this year?	Yes, I **am**./No, **I'm not**. Yes, she **is**./No, she **isn't**. Yes, they **are**./No, they **aren't**.	*Some verbs generally not used in the present continuous* have know like love want
Where **are** you **working** this month? What **is** she **doing** these days? Who **are** they **visiting** this week?	**I'm working** in Japan. She**'s teaching** at a university. They**'re visiting** their parents.	

A Complete these conversations using the present tense or the present continuous. Then practice with a partner.

1. A: Is anyone in your family looking for a job?
   B: Yes, my sister is. She .... (work) part time in a restaurant now, but she .... (look) for a job in a theater company. She .... (love) acting.

2. A: What is your brother doing these days?
   B: He .... (go) to college this semester. He .... (like) it a lot. He .... (study) mathematics.

3. A: Where do your parents live?
   B: They .... (live) in Chicago most of the time, but they .... (stay) in Florida this winter. They .... (have) a house there.

B ***Pair work*** Take turns asking the questions in part A or similar questions of your own. Give your own information when answering.

C ***Group work*** Take turns. Ask each student about his or her family. Then ask follow-up questions to get more information.

Topics to ask about

traveling
living abroad
taking a class
moving to a new home
going to college or high school
studying a foreign language
looking for a job

A: Is anyone in your family traveling right now?
B: Yes, my father is.
C: Where is he?
B: He's in Bangkok.
D: What's he doing there?
B: . . .

interchange 5

Family facts

Find out some interesting facts about your classmates' families. Turn to page IC-7.

6 SNAPSHOT

Source: The Family and Medical Leave Act

Talk about these questions.

Which of these facts surprises you?
Do women with children usually work in your country?
Do people often get divorced?
Do elderly people generally live with relatives?

7 CONVERSATION *Describing family life*

A Listen and practice.

Ryan: Look at this headline, Soo Mi.
Soo Mi: Wow! So many people in the United States get divorced!
Ryan: Is it the same in Korea?
Soo Mi: I don't think so. In Korea, some marriages break up, but most couples stay together.
Ryan: Do people get married young?
Soo Mi: Not really. Very few people get married before the age of 20.
Ryan: Hmm. Do women usually work after they get married?
Soo Mi: No, a lot of women stay home and take care of their families. But some work.

CLASS AUDIO ONLY

B Listen to the rest of the conversation.

What does Ryan say about families in the United States? Write down two things.

8 GRAMMAR FOCUS

Determiners

100%	All Nearly all Most	women with children work.
	Many A lot of Some	women stay home after they get married.
	Not many A few Few	couples stay together.
0%	No one	gets married before the age of 20.

A Rewrite these sentences using determiners. Then compare with a partner.

1. In Australia, 87% of married couples have children.
   ....
2. Six percent of 20- to 24-year-olds in the United States are divorced.
   ....
3. Thirty-five percent of the people in Germany live alone.
   ....
4. In China, 50% of women get married by the age of 22.
   ....

#35

B ***Pair work*** Rewrite the sentences in part A so that they are about your country. Then discuss your information with a partner.

In my country, only some married couples have children.

useful expressions

Is that right?
Do you think so? I think . . . .
I don't agree.
I don't think so.
It's different in my country.

9 WRITING

A Write about families in your country. Use some of your ideas from Exercise 8.

In my country, most people get married by the age of 30. Not many women work after they get married. Grandparents, parents, and children often live in the same house. . . .

B ***Group work*** Take turns reading your compositions. Then answer any questions from the group.

10 READING

The Changing Family

What kinds of problems do parents have in your country?

American families are changing. One important change is that most married women now work outside the home. What happens when both parents work? Read about the Morales family.

Judy and Steve Morales have three children: Josh, 12; Ben, 9; and Emily, 6. Steve is a computer programmer. This year, Judy is working again as a hospital administrator. The family needs the money, and Judy likes her job. Everything is going well, but there are also some problems.

Now that Judy is working, Steve has to help her more with the housework. He doesn't enjoy it, however.

Judy loves her work, but she feels tired and too busy. She also worries about the children. Judy has to work on Saturdays, so Steve and Judy don't have a lot of free time together.

Emily is having a great time in her after-school program. When Judy comes to pick her up, she doesn't want to leave.

Unfortunately, Ben's school doesn't have an after-school program. Right now, he's spending most afternoons by himself in front of the TV.

Josh is enjoying his new freedom after school. He's playing his music louder and spending more time on the phone. He's also doing a few household chores.

A Read the article. What are Steve's and Judy's problems? Complete the chart.

	Problems
1. Steve	....
2. Judy	....
3. Steve and Judy	....

B ***Pair work*** Talk about these questions.

1. Which of the problems above do you think is the most serious? Offer some solutions for that problem.
2. Which of the children are benefiting from Judy's working? Which one is not?

6 How often do you exercise?

1 SNAPSHOT

Top six sports and fitness activities for teenagers in the United States

MALES	FEMALES
1. Football	1. Swimming
2. Basketball	2. Basketball
3. Weight training	3. Bicycling
4. Jogging	4. Aerobics
5. Bicycling	5. Jogging
6. Swimming	6. Regular fitness program

Source: *America's Youth in the 1990s;* George H. Gallup International Institute

Talk about these questions.

Do males and females in your country enjoy any of these sports or activities?
Do you enjoy any of these or other sports or activities? Which ones?

2 WORD POWER *Sports and exercise*

A ***Pair work*** Which of these activities are popular with the following age groups? Check (✓) the activities. Then compare with a partner.

	Children	Teens	Young adults	Middle-aged people	Older people
aerobics	☐	☐	☐	☐	☐
baseball	☐	☐	☐	☐	☐
bicycling	☐	☐	☐	☐	☐
Rollerblading	☐	☐	☐	☐	☐
soccer	☐	☐	☐	☐	☐
swimming	☐	☐	☐	☐	☐
tennis	☐	☐	☐	☐	☐
weight training	☐	☐	☐	☐	☐
yoga	☐	☐	☐	☐	☐

A: I think aerobics are popular with teens.
B: And with young adults.

B ***Pair work*** Which of the activities above are used with *do*, *go*, or *play*?

do aerobics	*go bicycling*	*play baseball*
....	....	....
....	....	....

3 CONVERSATION *Describing routines*

A Listen and practice.

Marie: You're really fit, Paul. Do you exercise very much?
Paul: Well, I almost always get up very early, and I lift weights for an hour.
Marie: You're kidding!
Paul: No. And then I often go Rollerblading.
Marie: Wow! How often do you exercise like that?
Paul: About five times a week. What about you?
Marie: Oh, I hardly ever exercise. I usually just watch TV in my free time. I guess I'm a real couch potato!

CLASS AUDIO ONLY

B Listen to the rest of the conversation.

What else does Paul do in his free time?

4 GRAMMAR FOCUS

Adverbs of frequency

How often do you **usually** exercise?	Do you **ever** watch television in the evening?	100%	**always**
I lift weights **every day.**	Yes, I **almost always** watch TV after dinner.		**almost always**
I go jogging about **once a week.**	I **sometimes** watch TV before bed.		**usually**
I play basketball **twice a month.**	**Sometimes** I watch TV before bed.*		**often**
I exercise about **three times a year.**	I **seldom** watch TV in the evening.		**sometimes**
I don't exercise **very often/very much.**	No, I **never** watch TV.		**seldom**
			hardly ever
			almost never
	****Sometimes can begin a sentence.***	0%	**never**

A Put the adverbs in the correct place. Then practice with a partner.

1. A: What do you do on Saturday mornings? (usually)
   B: Nothing much. I sleep until noon. (almost always)
2. A: Do you go bicycling? (ever)
   B: Yeah, I go bicycling on Saturdays. (often)
3. A: How often do you play sports? (usually)
   B: Well, I play tennis. (twice a week)
4. A: What do you do after class? (usually)
   B: I go out with my classmates. (about three times a week)
5. A: How often do you exercise? (usually)
   B: I exercise. (seldom)

B ***Pair work*** Take turns asking the questions in part A. Give your own information when answering.

5 PRONUNCIATION *Sentence stress*

A Listen to the syllables stressed in each sentence. Notice that the adverbs of frequency are stressed. Then practice the sentences.

I hardly **ev**er do **yo**ga in the **morn**ing.
I **of**ten go **Ro**llerblading on **Sat**urdays.
I almost **al**ways play **ten**nis on **week**ends.

B ***Pair work*** Write four sentences about yourself using adverbs of frequency. Then take turns saying the sentences using the correct stress.

6 FITNESS POLL

A ***Group work*** Take a poll in your group. One person takes notes. Take turns asking each person these questions.

1. Do you have a regular fitness program? How often do you exercise?
2. Do you ever go to a gym? How often do you go? What do you do there?
3. Do you play any sports? How often do you play?
4. How often do you take long walks? Where do you go?
5. What else do you do to keep fit?

B ***Group work*** Study the results of the poll. Who in your group has a good fitness program?

7 LISTENING

CLASS AUDIO ONLY

Listen to what Ted, Wanda, and Kim like to do in the evening. Complete the chart.

	Favorite activity	How often?
Ted	....	....
Wanda	....	....
Kim	....	....

8 WRITING *Favorite activities*

A Write about your favorite activities.

I love to exercise. I usually work out every day. I get up early in the morning and go running for about an hour. Then I often go to the gym and do aerobics. Sometimes I go for a walk in the afternoon. About once a week, I play basketball.

B ***Group work*** Take turns reading your compositions. Then answer any questions from the group.

9 CONVERSATION *Describing exercise*

Listen and practice.

Rod: You're in great shape, Keith.
Do you work out at a gym?
Keith: Yeah, I do. I guess I'm a real fitness freak.
Rod: So, how often do you work out?
Keith: Well, I do aerobics every day after work.
And then I play racquetball.
Rod: Say, I like racquetball, too.
Keith: Oh, do you want to play sometime?
Rod: Uh, . . . how well do you play?
Keith: Pretty well, I guess.
Rod: Well, all right. But I'm not very good.
Keith: No problem, Rod. I won't play too hard.

10 LISTENING

CLASS AUDIO ONLY

Listen to John, Anne, and Phil discuss sports and exercise. Which one is a couch potato? a fitness freak? a sports fanatic?

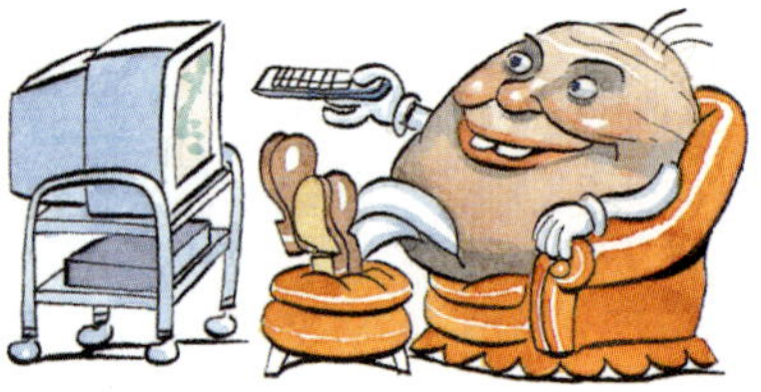
a couch potato

a fitness freak

a sports fanatic

1. ....
2. ....
3. ....

interchange 6

Fitness quiz

Find out how fit you are. Turn to page IC-8.

11 GRAMMAR FOCUS

Questions with how; short answers

How often do you work out?	Twice a week. Not very often.
How much time do you spend at the gym? **How long** do you spend working out?	Around two hours a day. I don't work out.
How well do you play racquetball?	Pretty well. About average, I guess. Not very well.
How good are you at sports?	I'm pretty good at sports. I guess I'm OK. Not too good.

A Complete these questions. Practice with a partner. Then write four more questions.

1. A: .... at volleyball?
   B: I guess I'm pretty good.
2. A: .... swim?
   B: Not very well, but I'd like to learn to swim better.
3. A: .... watch sports?
   B: Pretty often. About three or four times a week.
4. A: .... spend exercising?
   B: I spend about an hour every day.

B ***Group work*** Take turns asking the questions in part A and your own questions. Give your own information when answering.

Who in your group is a couch potato? a fitness freak? a sports fanatic?

12 READING

Smart Moves

Look at the statements in part A below. Which do you think are true?

It won't surprise fitness freaks to learn that aerobic exercise does more than raise the heart rate: It lifts the spirit and builds confidence. But many brain researchers believe that something else happens, too. Just as exercise makes the bones, muscles, heart, and lungs stronger, researchers think that it also strengthens important parts of the brain.

Research suggests that aerobic exercise helps you learn new things and remember old information better. Aerobic exercise sends more blood to the brain and it also feeds the brain with substances that develop new nerve connections. If the exercise has complicated movements like dance steps or basketball moves, the brain produces even more nerve connections – the more connections, the better the brain can process all kinds of information.

Scientists still don't fully understand the relationship between exercise and brain power. For the moment, people just have to trust that exercise is helping them to learn or remember. Scientific research clearly shows, however, that three or more workouts a week are good for you. A study in the *Journal of the American Medical Association*, for example, shows that walking four to five miles (6.5 to 8 km) an hour for 45 minutes five times a week helps you live longer. So don't be a couch potato. Get out there and do something!

A ***Pair work*** According to the article, which of these statements are probably true? Check (✓) the statements. What information helped you determine this? Underline the information in the article.

Exercise . . .

1. makes you feel happier. ☐
2. makes you feel more self-confident. ☐
3. strengthens the body. ☐
4. can increase your height. ☐
5. can help you learn things better. ☐
6. helps you remember things better. ☐
7. gives you better eyesight. ☐
8. helps you live longer. ☐

B ***Pair work*** Talk about these questions. Explain your answers.

1. Do you think that exercise helps people to learn and remember better?
2. Can you think of other benefits from exercise?
3. What benefits are most important to you?

7 We had a great time!

1 SNAPSHOT

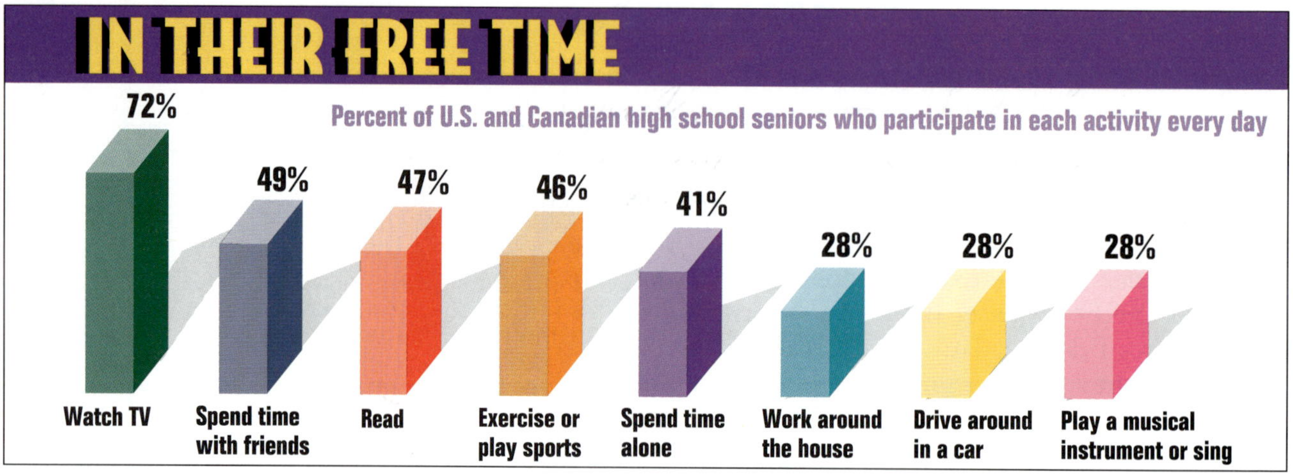

Source: University of Michigan, Institute for Social Research

Complete these tasks and talk about them.

Which of these activities do you do every day?
List three other activities you like to do almost every day.
Put the activities you do in order: from the most interesting to the least interesting.

2 CONVERSATION *The weekend*

A Listen and practice.

Chris: So, what did you do this weekend, Kate?
Kate: Oh, Diane and I went for a drive in the country on Saturday.
Chris: That sounds nice. Where did you go?
Kate: We drove to the lake and had a picnic. We had a great time! How about you? Did you do anything special?
Chris: Not really. I just worked on my car all day.
Kate: That old thing! Why don't you just buy a new one?
Chris: But then what would I do every weekend?

CLASS AUDIO ONLY

B Listen to Kate talk about her activities on Sunday.

1. What did she do?
2. Where did she go?

3 GRAMMAR FOCUS

Past tense

Did you **stay** home on Sunday?	Yes, I **did**. I **watched** a football game on TV. No, I **didn't**. I **invited** friends out to dinner.	***Regular verbs*** invite → invit**ed** work → work**ed** stay → stay**ed** study → stud**ied**
What **did** you **do** on Saturday?	I **worked** on my car. I **stayed** home and **studied**.	
Did you **do** anything special?	Yes, I **did**. I **drove** to the lake. No, I **didn't**. I **had** to baby-sit.	***Irregular verbs*** drive → **drove** go → **went** have → **had** see → **saw** spend → **spent**
Where **did** you **go** on Sunday?	I **saw** a good movie. I **went** to a concert.	

For a list of irregular past forms and pronunciation rules for regular past forms, see the appendix at the back of the book.

A Complete these conversations. Then practice with a partner.

1. A: .... you .... (go) out on Friday night?
   B: No, I .... I .... (invite) friends over, and I .... (cook) dinner for them.
2. A: How .... you .... (spend) your last birthday?
   B: I .... (have) a party. Everyone .... (enjoy) it, but the neighbors .... (complain) about the noise.
3. A: What .... you .... (do) last night?
   B: I .... (go) to the new Tom Cruise film. I .... (love) it!
4. A: .... you .... (do) anything special over the weekend?
   B: Yes, I .... I .... (go) shopping. Unfortunately, I .... (spend) all my money. Now I'm broke!

B ***Pair work*** Take turns asking the questions in part A. Give your own information when answering.

4 PRONUNCIATION *Reduced forms of* did you

A Listen and practice. Notice how **did you** is reduced in the following questions.

[dɪdʒə]
Did you have a good time?

[wədɪdʒə]
What did you do last night?

B ***Pair work*** Practice the questions in the grammar box in Exercise 3. Pay attention to the pronunciation of **did you**.

5 WORD POWER Collocation

A Find two other words or phrases from the list that are usually paired with each verb.

an art exhibition	a vacation	a party	a trip	shopping
a lot of fun	the dishes	dancing	a play	the laundry

did	*housework*	the laundry	the dishes
went	*swimming*	dancing	shopping
had	*a good time*	a party	a lot of fun
saw	*a movie*	an art exhibition	a play
took	*a day off*	a vacation	a trip

B Write five sentences using words from the list.

I saw a movie last weekend.

6 ANY QUESTIONS?

Group work Take turns. One student makes a statement about the weekend. Other students ask questions. Each student answers at least four questions.

A: I went dancing on Saturday night.
B: **Where** did you go?
A: To the Rock-it Club.
C: **Who** did you go with?
A: I went with my brother.
D: **What time** did you go?
A: We went at around 10:00.
E: **How** did you like it?
A: . . .

7 LISTENING

CLASS AUDIO ONLY

A Listen to John and Laura describe what they did last night. Check (✓) the correct information about each person.

CLASS AUDIO ONLY

B Listen to the conversation again. What did each person do? Take notes. Then take turns telling their stories to a partner.

	John	Laura
had a boring time	☐	☐
had a good time	☐	☐
met someone interesting	☐	☐
got home late	☐	☐

8 CONVERSATION On vacation

Listen and practice.

Mike: Hi, Celia! How was your trip to the United States?
Celia: It was terrific. I really enjoyed it.
Mike: Great. How long were you away?
Celia: I was there for about three weeks.
Mike: That's a long time! Was the weather OK?
Celia: Yes, most of the time. But it snowed a lot in Chicago.
Mike: So, what was the best thing about your trip?
Celia: Oh, that's difficult to say. But I guess I liked Nashville the best.

9 GRAMMAR FOCUS

Past tense of be

Were you away last week?	Yes, I **was**.	***Contractions***
Was your brother away . . . ?	No, he **wasn't**.	was not = was**n't**
Were you and your sister away . . . ?	Yes, we **were**.	were not = were**n't**
Were your parents away . . . ?	No, they **weren't**.	
How long **were** you away?	I **was** away for three weeks.	
How **was** your vacation?	It **was** terrific!	

Complete these conversations. Then practice with a partner.

1. A: How long .... your parents in Europe?
   B: They .... there for a month.
   A: .... they in London the whole time?
   B: No, they .... They also went to Paris and Madrid.

2. A: .... you away last weekend?
   B: Yes, I .... I .... in San Francisco.
   A: How .... it?
   B: It .... great!
   A: How .... the weather?
   B: Oh, it .... foggy and cool as usual.

3. A: I .... in Istanbul last summer.
   B: Really? How long .... you there?
   A: For six weeks.
   B: .... you there on business or on vacation?
   A: I .... there on business.

10 VACATIONS

A ***Group work*** Take turns talking about vacations. Ask these questions and others of your own.

Where did you spend your last vacation?
How long were you away?
Were you with your family?
What did you do there?
How was the weather? the food?
Did you buy anything?
Do you want to go there again?

B ***Class activity*** Who in your group had the most interesting vacation? Tell the class who and why.

interchange 7

Vacation photos

Use the vacation photos to tell a story. Student A turns to page IC-9. Student B turns to page IC-10.

11 LISTENING

CLASS AUDIO ONLY

Listen to Jason and Barbara talk about their vacations. Complete the chart.

	Vacation place	Enjoyed it? Yes	No	Reason(s)
Jason	....	☐	☐	....
Barbara	....	☐	☐	....

12 WRITING

A Read this postcard.

Dear Richard,
Greetings from Acapulco! I'm having a great time! Yesterday I went on a tour of the city, and today I went shopping. I bought some beautiful jewelry. Oh, and last night, I heard some Mariachi singers on the street. They were terrific. That's all for now.

Love,
Kathy

B ***Pair work*** Write a postcard to a partner about your last vacation or an interesting place you visited recently. Then exchange postcards.

13 READING *Vacation postcards*

Look at the pictures. What do you think each person did on his or her vacation?

Paula,

I can't believe my trip is over. I arrived in Egypt just two weeks ago! I was with a group from the university. We went to the desert to dig in some old ruins. I didn't find anything, but I learned a lot. I'm tired, but I loved every minute of my trip.

Take care, Margaret

Hi, Luis!

My Hawaiian vacation just ended, and I am very relaxed! I spent my whole vacation at a spa in Koloa, Kauai. Every day for a week I exercised, did yoga, meditated, and ate vegetarian food. I also went swimming and snorkeling. I feel fantastic!

Love, Sue

Dear Michael,

Alaska is terrific! I was just on a trip in the Arctic National Wildlife Refuge. There were six people on the trip. We hiked for ten days. Then we took rafts to the Arctic Ocean. I saw a lot of wildlife. Now I'm going to Anchorage. See you in 3 weeks!

Kevin

A Read the postcards. Then check (✓) the statements that are true.

- ☐ 1. Margaret had a very relaxing vacation.
- ☐ 2. Margaret enjoyed her vacation.
- ☐ 3. Sue was in Hawaii for two weeks.
- ☐ 4. Sue got a lot of exercise.
- ☐ 5. Kevin spent his vacation alone.
- ☐ 6. Kevin's vacation is over.

B ***Group work*** Talk about these questions. Explain your answers.

1. Which person learned a lot on vacation?
2. Who had a vacation that was full of adventure?
3. Who had a very relaxing vacation?
4. Which vacation sounds the most interesting to you?

8 How do you like the neighborhood?

1 WORD POWER *Places*

A Match the words and the definitions. Then practice asking the questions with a partner.

What's a . . . ?	*It's a place where you . . .*
1. barber shop	a. wash and dry clothes.
2. laundromat	b. buy food.
3. library	c. buy cards and paper.
4. stationery store	d. get a haircut.
5. travel agency	e. see a movie or play.
6. grocery store	f. make reservations for a trip.
7. theater	g. borrow books.

B ***Pair work*** Write definitions for these places.

bank	coffee shop	drugstore	gym	post office
bookstore	dance club	gas station	hotel	restaurant

It's a place where you keep your money. (bank)

C ***Group work*** Read your definitions in groups. Can others guess what each place is?

2 CONVERSATION *The neighborhood*

Listen and practice.

Jack: Excuse me. I'm your new neighbor, Jack. I just moved in.
Woman: Oh. Yes?
Jack: I'm looking for a grocery store. Are there any around here?
Woman: Yes, there are some on Pine Street.
Jack: OK. And is there a laundromat near here?
Woman: Well, I think there's one across from the shopping center.
Jack: Thank you.
Woman: By the way, there's a barber shop in the shopping center, too.
Jack: A barber shop?

3 GRAMMAR FOCUS

There is, there are; one, any, some

Is there a laundromat near here?
Yes, **there is.** There's **one** across from the shopping center.
No, **there isn't**, but there's **one** next to the library.

Are there any grocery stores around here?
Yes, **there are.** There are **some** on Pine Street.
No, **there aren't**, but there are **some** on Third Avenue.

Prepositions
on
next to
across from/opposite
in front of
in back of/behind
near/close to
between
on the corner of

A Write questions about these places in the neighborhood map below.

a bank	a department store	a gym	a laundromat	a post office
gas stations	grocery stores	hotels	a pay phone	restaurants

Is there a pay phone around here?
Are there any restaurants on Maple Avenue?

B ***Pair work*** Ask and answer the questions you wrote in part A.

A: Is there a pay phone around here?
B: Yes, there is. There's one across from the post office.

4 PRONUNCIATION *Reduced forms of* there is/there are

Listen and practice. Notice how **there is** and **there are** are reduced in conversation.

There's a gym across from the shopping center.
There's a bookstore near the laundromat.

There are some restaurants on Elm Street.
There are some grocery stores across from the post office.

5 IN YOUR NEIGHBORHOOD

Group work Take turns asking and answering questions about places like these in your neighborhood.

a bookstore	dance clubs	a coffee shop	a music store	stationery stores
a gym	drugstores	movie theaters	a pay phone	a travel agency

A: Is there a good bookstore in your neighborhood?
B: . . .
A: And are there any drugstores?
B: . . .

useful expressions

Sorry, I don't know.
I'm not sure, but I think . . . .
Of course. There's one . . . .

6 LISTENING

CLASS AUDIO ONLY

Some hotel guests are asking about places to visit in the neighborhood. Complete the chart.

Place	Location	Interesting? Yes	Interesting? No
Hard Rock Cafe	....	☐	☐
Science Museum	....	☐	☐
Aquarium	....	☐	☐

7 SNAPSHOT

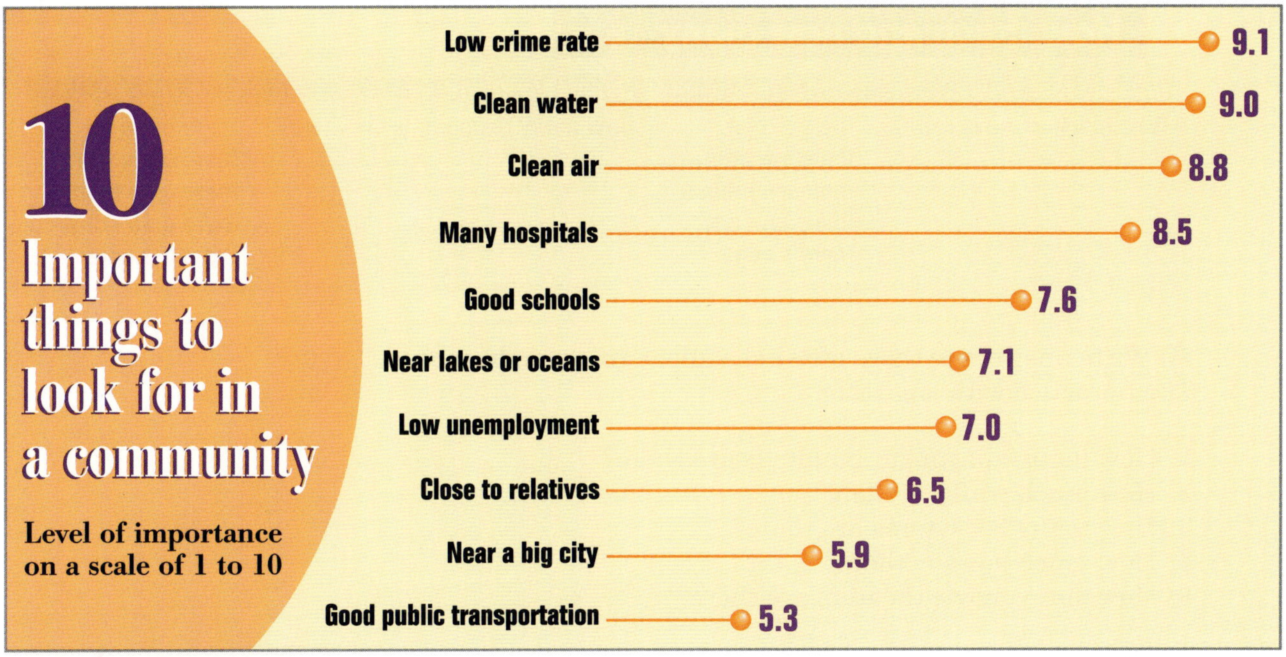

Source: *Money* Magazine

Complete these tasks and talk about them.

What is important to you in a community? Rank the features above from the most important (1) to the least important (10).

List three other things you think are important in a community.

8 CONVERSATION *Describing neighborhoods*

A Listen and practice.

Dan: Where do you live, Kim?
Kim: I live in an apartment downtown.
Dan: Oh, that's convenient, but . . . how much crime is there?
Kim: Not much. But there is a *lot* of traffic. I can't stand the noise sometimes! Where do you live?
Dan: I have a house in the suburbs.
Kim: Oh, I bet it's really quiet. But is there much to do there?
Dan: No, not much. In fact, nothing ever really happens. That's the trouble.
Kim: Hey. Let's trade places one weekend!
Dan: OK. Great idea!

CLASS AUDIO ONLY

B Listen to the rest of the conversation.

What do Dan and Kim say about restaurants in their neighborhoods?

9 *GRAMMAR FOCUS*

How much *and* how many

Uncountable nouns		*Countable nouns*	
How much crime is there?	There's **a lot**. There's **a little**. There **isn't much**. There **isn't any**. There's **none**.	**How many** restaurants are there?	There are **a lot**. There are **a few**. There **aren't many**. There **aren't any**. There are **none**.

A Write answers to these questions about your neighborhood. Then practice with a partner.

1. How many apartment buildings are there? ....
2. How much traffic is there? ....
3. How many bookstores are there? ....
4. How much noise is there? ....
5. How many movie theaters are there? ....

B ***Pair work*** Write questions like those in part A about these topics. Then ask and answer the questions.

crime   parks   pollution   restaurants   schools   stores

interchange 8

Neighborhood survey

Compare two neighborhoods in your city. Turn to page IC-11.

10 *WRITING*

A ***Group work*** Talk about where you live. Discuss these questions in groups.

Do you live in a house or an apartment?
Where is it?
How many rooms are there?
How much noise is there?
Are there any good restaurants nearby?
How many clubs/theaters/gyms are there in your neighborhood?
Is there any public transportation near your home?
How do you like it there?

B Write a paragraph about where you live. Use the information you discussed in part A.

I live in a big apartment building in the city. There are two bedrooms, a living room, a dining room, and a kitchen. There's a lot of noise in my neighborhood because there's a dance club across from my building. . . .

11 READING

City Scenes

What are cities like in your country?

In many countries around the world, more and more people live in cities. Cities share many characteristics, but are also different from country to country.

Mexico Mexico's cities are modern but have traditional Indian and Spanish influences. The most important buildings are around a central square, which also serves as a place to meet with friends. There are outdoor marketplaces, where people can find almost anything they need. On Sundays, parks are a popular place for family outings. Many people move to Mexico City from rural areas. It has a lot of excitement, but also lots of traffic and air pollution.

Japan Japan's cities also have a mix of traditional and modern characteristics. There are tall office and apartment buildings as well as traditional wooden houses. Many people prefer to live near the center of cities, but because houses there are expensive, they often commute from suburbs. Traffic, pollution, and crowds are problems. However, there is little crime, and even very crowded cities have many parks and gardens.

Australia Although 80% of Australians live near cities, the cities are not as large as those in some other countries. Most people live in houses in suburbs – not in apartments. The suburbs usually have their own churches, schools, and shopping centers. They also have recreational facilities. In large cities, like Sydney, the suburbs are often far from the center of town. Because many people commute to work, traffic is slow and there are many traffic jams.

A Read the article and complete the chart. Write one positive feature and one negative feature of cities in the countries described.

	Positive	Negative
1. Mexico	....	....
2. Japan	....	....
3. Australia	....	....

B ***Pair work*** Find five characteristics of the cities above that are also true of cities in your country.

Review of Units 5–8

1 DO YOU DANCE?

A ***Class activity*** Does anyone in your class do these things? How often and how well do they do them? Go around the class and find one person for each activity.

	Name	How often?	How well?
dance	....	....	....
play basketball	....	....	....
do karate	....	....	....
play computer games	....	....	....
swim	....	....	....
play the piano	....	....	....

A: Do you dance?
B: Yes, I do.
A: How often do you go dancing?
B: Every weekend.
A: And how well do you dance?
B: Actually, not very well. But I enjoy it!

B ***Group work*** Tell your group what you found out.

2 LISTENING

CLASS AUDIO ONLY

A A thief robbed a house on Saturday. Detective Dobbs is questioning Frankie. The pictures show what Frankie did on Saturday. Listen to their conversation. Are Frankie's answers true (**T**) or false (**F**)?

1:00 P.M. **T F**

3:00 P.M. **T F**

5:00 P.M. **T F**

6:00 P.M. **T F**

8:00 P.M. **T F**

10:30 P.M. **T F**

B ***Pair work*** Answer these questions.

1. What did Frankie do after he cleaned the house?
2. Where did he go? What did he do? When did he come home?

3 WHAT CAN YOU REMEMBER?

A ***Pair work*** Talk about what you did yesterday. Take turns asking these questions. Give as much information as possible.

What time did you get up yesterday?
What did you wear?
Were you late for class?
Did you meet anyone interesting?
How many phone calls did you make?
Did you drive or take the bus anywhere?
Did you buy anything?
How much money did you spend yesterday?
Did you watch TV? What programs did you watch?
Did you do any exercise?
Were you in bed before midnight?
What time did you go to sleep?

B ***Group work*** Close your books. Take turns. How many questions can you ask?

4 ROLE PLAY *What's it like?*

Student A: Imagine you are a visitor in your city. You want to find out more about it. Ask the questions in the box.

Student B: You are a resident of your city. A visitor wants to find out more about it. Answer the visitor's questions.

Change roles and try the role play again.

Questions to ask

What's it like to live here?
How much unemployment is there?
How much crime is there?
How many good schools are there?
Is traffic a problem?
What's public transportation like?
Are there many places to shop? Where?

5 WHAT'S GOING ON?

CLASS AUDIO ONLY

A Listen to the sounds of four people doing different things. What do you think each person is doing?

What's going on?	
1.	**3.** ....
2.	**4.** ....

B ***Pair work*** Compare your answers with a partner.

A: In number 1, someone is shaving.
B: I don't think so. I think someone is . . . .

9 What does he look like?

1 WORD POWER *Appearance*

A Look at these expressions. Can you add three more words or expressions to describe people? Write them in the box below.

Height

short | fairly short | medium height | pretty tall | tall

Age

young | middle aged | elderly

Looks

handsome | good-looking | pretty

Hair

straight black hair | curly red hair | short blond hair

long brown hair | bald | a mustache and beard

Other words or expressions

....

....

....

B ***Pair work*** Choose at least four expressions to describe yourself and your partner. Then compare. Do you agree?

A: You have curly blond hair and a beard.
You're young and good-looking.
B: I agree! / I don't agree. My hair isn't very curly.

Me	My partner
....	....
....	....
....	....
....	....

2 CONVERSATION Describing someone

Listen and practice.

Clerk: Good afternoon. Can I help you?
Jean: Yes, I'm looking for someone. His name is Martin Bock. I'm afraid I missed him.
Clerk: Well, what does he look like?
Jean: Let's see. He's about 35, I guess. He's pretty tall, with red hair.
Clerk: Oh, are you Jean Taylor?
Jean: Yes, that's right!
Clerk: He asked for you a few minutes ago. I think he's in the restaurant.
Jean: Thanks. I'll go and look for him.

3 GRAMMAR FOCUS

Questions for describing people

General appearance	
What does he **look like?**	He's pretty tall, with red hair.
Does he wear glasses?	Yes, he does.
Does he have a mustache?	No, he doesn't.
Age	
How old is he?	He's about 25. He's in his twenties.

Hair	
What color is her hair?	Light brown. She has dark brown hair.
How long is her hair?	It's medium length.
Height	
How tall is she?	She's fairly short. She's 152 cm (five feet).

A Write questions to match these statements. Then compare with a partner.

1. .... ? My brother is 26.
2. .... ? I'm 173 cm (five feet eight).
3. .... ? Julia has brown hair.
4. .... ? No, she wears contact lenses.
5. .... ? He's tall and very handsome.
6. .... ? I have brown eyes.

B ***Pair work*** Write five questions about your teacher's or a classmate's appearance. Then take turns asking and answering your questions.

What color is Aki's hair?

4 WHO IS IT?

CLASS AUDIO ONLY

A Listen to the speakers describe these people. Number the people from 1 to 5.

B ***Pair work*** Choose a person in your class. Don't tell your partner who it is. Take turns. Ask questions to guess the person your partner chose.

A: Is it a man or a woman?
B: A man.
A: How tall is he?
B: He's fairly short.
A: What color is his hair?
B: . . .

interchange 9

Find the differences

Compare two pictures of a party. Student A turns to page IC-12. Student B turns to page IC-14.

5 WRITING

A Write a description of a person in your class. Don't put the person's name on it.

He's in his twenties. He's quite good-looking. He's tall, and he has short blond hair. He's wearing a red shirt, a black jacket, and khaki pants. He's sitting next to the window.

B ***Group work*** Read your description to the group. Can they guess who you are describing?

6 SNAPSHOT

Talk about these questions.

Which of these items are in style now? out of style?
What are three more things that are in style today?
What are two things you wear now that you didn't wear five years ago?

7 CONVERSATION *Identifying people*

A Listen and practice.

Sarah: Hi, Raoul! Good to see you! Where's Margaret?
Raoul: Oh, she couldn't make it. She went to a concert with Alex.
Sarah: Oh! Well, why don't you go and talk to Judy? She doesn't know anyone here.
Raoul: Judy? Which one is she? Is she the woman wearing glasses over there?
Sarah: No, she's the tall one in jeans. She's standing near the window.
Raoul: Oh, I'd like to meet her.

CLASS AUDIO ONLY

B Listen to the rest of the conversation.

Can you label Kevin, Michiko, Rosa, and John in the picture?

8 GRAMMAR FOCUS

Modifiers with participles and prepositions

		Participles
Who's Raoul?	He's **the man**	**wearing** glasses.
Which one is Raoul?	He's **the one**	**talking** to Sarah.
		Prepositions
Who's Sarah?	She's **the woman**	**with** the short black hair.
Which one is Judy?	She's **the tall one**	**in** jeans.
Who are the Smiths?	They're **the people**	**next to** the window.
Which ones are the Smiths?	They're **the ones**	**on** the couch.

A Rewrite these statements using modifiers with participles or prepositions. Then compare with a partner.

1. Jim is the tall guy. He's wearing glasses.
   Jim is the tall guy wearing glasses.
2. Bob and Louise are the good-looking couple. They're talking to Jim.
   ....
3. Lynne is the young woman. She's in a T-shirt and jeans.
   ....
4. Maria is the attractive woman. She's sitting to the left of Carlos.
   ....
5. Tom is the serious-looking person. He's listening to Maria.
   ....

B *Pair work* Complete these questions and add two questions of your own. Use the names of people in your class. Then take turns asking and answering the questions.

1. Who is .... ?
2. Which one is .... ?
3. Who's the man sitting next to .... ?
4. Who's the woman wearing .... ?
5. .... ?
6. .... ?

9 PRONUNCIATION *Contrastive stress*

A Listen and practice. Notice how the stress changes to emphasize a contrast.

A: Is Raoul the one wearing the red **shírt**?
B: No, he's the one wearing the **bláck** shirt.

A: Is Judy the short one in **jéans**?
B: No, she's the **táll** one in jeans.

B Mark the stress changes in these conversations. Listen and check. Then practice the conversations.

1. A: Is Rose the one sitting next to Kate?
   B: No, she's the one standing next to Kate.
2. A: Is Brian the man on the couch?
   B: No, Brian's the man behind the couch.

10 READING

Hip-Hop Fashions

**What kinds of clothing styles do you like to wear?
Do you like to "dress up" or "dress down"?**

Teenagers who listen to the same music often have a common "look." One hot style in music and fashion is hip-hop. Hip-hop is a type of urban music with a heavy beat. The lyrics are very important in this music. Hip-hop fashions are large or loose-fitting street clothes. The style includes baggy jeans, sweatshirts, hiking boots, and baseball caps (usually worn backward). However, teens add other clothing items like flannel shirts, jackets with sports logos, and athletic shoes. In the hip-hop style, boys and girls dress the same.

African American kids in Detroit and Chicago first made hip-hop fashions popular – they wore baggy street clothes to dance clubs. Then North American and European bands also began wearing this style. These bands influenced one another's music and clothing. This mixture made hip-hop into an international fashion sensation.

Hip-hop is now a teen fashion from Britain to Japan. Melanie Borrow, 17, of Manchester, England, says, "My pride and joy in life are my Levi's jeans." In Japan, hip-hop is replacing the usual outfit for teenage girls: blouses and skirts with cartoon characters on them. And in the United States, teens spend a lot of money on hip-hop fashions. David Bowen, 17, of Evanston, Illinois, has five pairs of hiking boots at $100 each. Bowen says, "They're popular because a lot of hip-hop performers wear them. They even rap about them."

A Read the article. Then look at these pictures and label them. According to the article, which of the clothing items are hip-hop fashions? Check (✓) the correct items.

..*baggy jeans*... ☐

.... ☐

.... ☐

.... ☐

.... ☐

.... ☐

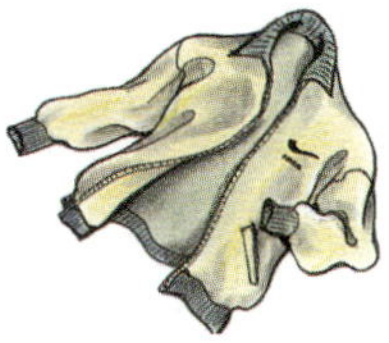
.... ☐

.... ☐

.... ☐

.... ☐

B ***Pair work*** Talk about these questions.

1. Do you ever listen to urban or hip-hop music?
2. Do you ever wear hip-hop fashions? Describe what you wear.
3. What do you wear when you dress up or dress down?

10 Have you ever ridden a camel?

1 SNAPSHOT

Talk about these questions.

Which of these activities would you like to try? Why?
What are three unusual things you can do in your city or country?

2 CONVERSATION *Going out*

A Listen and practice.

Ted: Are you enjoying your trip to New Orleans?
Brenda: Oh, yes. I really like it here.
Ted: Would you like to do something tonight?
Brenda: Sure. I'd love to.
Ted: Let's see. Have you been to a jazz club yet?
Brenda: Yes. I've already been to several clubs here.
Ted: OK. What about an evening riverboat tour?
Brenda: Uh, actually, I've gone twice this week.
Ted: So, what *do* you want to do?
Brenda: Well, I haven't been to the theater in a long time.
Ted: Oh, OK. I hear there's a terrific show at the Saenger Theater.
Brenda: Great! Let's make a reservation.

CLASS AUDIO ONLY **B** Listen to Ted call the Saenger Theater.

1. What's playing tonight?
2. Where is the theater?

3 GRAMMAR FOCUS

Present perfect; already, yet

The present perfect is formed with the verb **have** *+ the past participle form of a verb.*

Have you **been** to a jazz club?	Yes, **I've already been** to several.
Have they **seen** the play?	No, they **haven't seen** it **yet**.
Has she **gone** on a riverboat tour?	Yes, she**'s gone** twice this week.
Has he **called** his parents lately?	No, he **hasn't called** them.

Regular past participles

call → call**ed**
hike → hike**d**
jog → jogg**ed**
try → tri**ed**

Irregular past participles

be → **been**
do → **done**
eat → **eaten**
go → **gone**
have → **had**
make → **made**
see → **seen**

Contractions

I have = **I've**
have not = have**n't**
she has = she**'s**
has not = has**n't**

For a list of irregular past participles, see the appendix at the back of the book.

A How many times have you done these things in the past week? Write your answers. Then compare with a partner.

1. clean the house
2. make your bed
3. cook dinner
4. do laundry
5. wash the dishes
6. go grocery shopping

useful expressions

once
twice
three times
every day

I've cleaned the house once this week.

OR

I haven't cleaned the house this week.

B Complete these conversations using the present perfect. Then practice with a partner.

1. A: Have you done much exercise this week?
   B: Yes, I .... already .... to aerobics class four times. (be)
2. A: Have you played any sports this month?
   B: No, I .... the time. (have)
3. A: How many movies have you been to this month?
   B: Actually, I .... any yet. (see)
4. A: Have you been to any interesting parties lately?
   B: No, I .... to any parties for a while. (go)
5. A: Have you called any friends today?
   B: Yes, I .... already .... three calls. (make)
6. A: How many times have you gone out to eat this week?
   B: I .... at fast-food restaurants a couple of times. (eat)

C ***Pair work*** Take turns asking the questions in part B. Give your own information when answering.

4 CONVERSATION *Describing events*

A Listen and practice.

David Copperfield

Dave: So, how was your weekend?
Sue: Oh, really good. I went to see David Copperfield.
Dave: The magician?
Sue: That's right. Have you ever seen him?
Dave: Yes, I have. I saw his show in Las Vegas last year. He's terrific.
Sue: Yeah. He does some incredible things.
Dave: Have you ever been to Las Vegas?
Sue: No, I've never been there.
Dave: You should go sometime. It's an interesting city, and the hotels are wonderful.

B Have you ever seen a magician? When? Where? What did you think of the magician?

5 GRAMMAR FOCUS

Present perfect and past tense

Use the present perfect for an indefinite time in the past. Use the past tense for a specific event in the past.

Have you ever **seen** a magic show?	Yes, I **have**.	I **saw** a magic show last year.
	No, I **haven't**.	But my sister **saw** David Copperfield.
Have you ever **been** to Las Vegas?	Yes, I **have**.	I **went** there in September.
	No, I **haven't**.	**I've** never **been** there.

A Complete these conversations. Use the present perfect and the past tense of the verbs given and short answers. Then practice with a partner.

1. A: .... you ever .... skiing? (go)
   B: Yes, I .... I .... skiing once in Colorado.
2. A: .... you ever .... something valuable? (lose)
   B: No, I .... But my brother .... his camera on a trip once.
3. A: .... you ever .... a traffic ticket? (get)
   B: Yes, I .... Once I .... a ticket and had to pay $50.
4. A: .... you ever .... a body-building competition? (see)
   B: Yes, I .... I .... the National Championships this year.
5. A: .... you ever .... late for an important appointment? (be)
   B: No, I .... But my sister .... 30 minutes late for her wedding!

B ***Pair work*** Take turns asking the questions in part A. Give your own information when answering.

6 PRONUNCIATION Have

A Listen and practice. In questions, **have** is usually reduced to /həv/. In short answers, **have** is not reduced.

A: **Have** you ever been in a traffic accident?
B: Yes, I have.

A: **Have** you ever eaten Greek food?
B: No, I haven't.

B ***Pair work*** Write four questions like those in part A. Take turns asking and answering the questions. Pay attention to the pronunciation of **have**.

7 LISTENING

CLASS AUDIO ONLY

Listen to Clarice and Karl talk about interesting things they've done recently. Complete the chart.

	Where he/she went	Why he/she liked it
Clarice	....	....
Karl	....	....

8 WORD POWER Collocation

A Find two words or phrases in the list that are usually paired with each verb.

a camel	a hill	kiwi fruit	a mountain	rice wine	a truck
goat's milk	your keys	a motorcycle	raw fish	a sports car	your wallet

climb	....	....
drink	....	....
drive	....	....
eat	....	....
lose	....	....
ride	....	....

B Write the past participle forms of the verbs above. Then compare with a partner.

9 HAVE YOU EVER . . . ?

A *Group work* Ask your classmates questions about each of the things in Exercise 8. Take notes on the answers.

A: Have you ever ridden a camel?
B: Yes, I have.
A: Really? Where were you?
B: . . .

B *Class activity* Tell the class one interesting thing you learned about a classmate.

10 WRITING *I've never . . . .*

A Write a paragraph describing something that you've never done but would like to do. Explain why you want to do it.

I've never gone white-water rafting. I'd like to because it sounds exciting. My brother was on vacation in Canada two years ago and decided to try it. . . .

interchange 10

Lifestyles survey

Is your lifestyle easygoing and relaxed or busy and fast-paced? Turn to page IC-13.

B *Pair work* Exchange your compositions. Take turns asking and answering questions with a partner.

11 *READING*

Taking the Risk

Have you ever participated in a risky sport? What was it?

Sports World magazine spoke with Jenny Adams, Tom Barker, and Ray Lee about risky sports.

SW: Hang gliding is a dangerous sport. Jenny, what do you enjoy about the sport, and have you ever had an accident?

Jenny: No, I've never been seriously injured. Maybe I've just been lucky. Once, my glider turned upside down, and I lost control. I almost crashed, but I parachuted away just in time. And I've always felt hang gliding is quite safe – though landing is sometimes difficult. But it's fantastic to be able to fly like a bird!

SW: Tom, you've been mountain climbing for years now. What are some of the dangers that you've experienced?

Tom: High altitudes are hard on the human body. I've experienced lack of oxygen, tiredness, and dehydration. I've lived through storms, avalanches, and strong winds. But that's what I like about mountain climbing – overcoming danger.

SW: What exactly are the bends, Ray? And have you ever experienced them while scuba diving?

Ray: You get the bends when you've been deep under water. If you come up out of the water too quickly, bubbles form in your blood. The bends can be serious, and they can even cause death. But the bends are rare. Scuba diving isn't really dangerous. And it lets you explore another world.

A Read the article. What do Jenny, Tom, and Ray enjoy about the sports they describe? What is dangerous about each sport? Complete the chart.

	Sport	What they enjoy	The danger(s)
1. Jenny	....	....	....
2. Tom	....	....	....
3. Ray	....	....	....

B ***Pair work*** Talk about these questions.

1. Have you ever tried any of the sports described? What was it like?
2. Which of the sports would you like to try? Why?

11 It's a very exciting city!

1 WORD POWER *Adjectives*

A ***Pair work*** Match each word in column A with its opposite in column B. Then add two more pairs of adjectives to the list.

A	*B*
1. beautiful	a. boring
2. big	b. dangerous
3. cheap	c. dirty
4. clean	d. expensive
5. hot	e. stressful
6. interesting	f. small
7. safe	g. ugly
8. relaxing	h. cold
9.	i. ....
10.	j. ....

B Choose four adjectives from part A that describe your city. Then compare with a partner.

2 CONVERSATION *Describing cities*

A Listen and practice.

Linda: Where in Canada are you from, Ken?
Ken: I'm from Toronto.
Linda: Oh, I've never been there. What's it like?
Ken: It's a fairly big city, but it's not *too* big. The nightlife is good, too.
Linda: Is it expensive there?
Ken: No, it's not too bad.
Linda: And what's the weather like in Toronto?
Ken: Well, it's pretty cold in the winter, and very hot and humid in the summer. It's nice in the spring and fall, though.

CLASS AUDIO ONLY **B** Listen to the rest of the conversation.

What does Ken say about entertainment in Toronto?

3 GRAMMAR FOCUS

Adverbs and adjectives; conjunctions

It's a **very** exciting city. It's **too** expensive, **however.**
It's **not very** exciting. It's **really** beautiful, **though.**
It's a **fairly** big city, **but** it's **not too** big.
It's **pretty** safe, **and** it's **very** friendly.

A Match the questions with the answers. Then practice the conversations.

1. What's Hong Kong like? Is it an interesting place? ....
2. Do you like your hometown? ....
3. What's Sydney like? I've never been there. ....
4. Have you ever been to São Paulo? ....

a. Oh, really? It's beautiful, and it's very clean. It has a great harbor and beautiful beaches.
b. Yes, many times. It's a very modern city. It's too hot in the summer, though.
c. Yes, it is. It's very exciting. It's really crowded, however.
d. No, I hate it. It's not too small, but it's pretty boring. That's why I moved away.

B ***Pair work*** What do you think of these cities? Take turns describing them.

"San Francisco is a really exciting city, and it's very clean."

4 LISTENING

CLASS AUDIO ONLY

Listen to Joyce and Nick talk about their hometowns. What do they say? Check (✓) the correct boxes.

	Big?		Interesting?		Expensive?		Beautiful?	
	Yes	No	Yes	No	Yes	No	Yes	No
1. Joyce	☐	☐	☐	☐	☐	☐	☐	☐
2. Nick	☐	☐	☐	☐	☐	☐	☐	☐

5 HOME SWEET HOME

Group work Take turns. Ask one student about his or her hometown. Then ask follow-up questions to get more information.

What's your city like?

Is it an interesting place?
Is it very big?
Is it safe?
Is it clean?
Is it very expensive?
What's the nightlife like?
What's the weather like?
Do you like it there?

6 WRITING

Pair work Think of an interesting city in your country. Write a short composition about it. Then exchange compositions. Can your partner suggest any information to add?

My favorite city in the United States is Santa Fe. It's in New Mexico. It's an old city with lots of interesting Native American and Spanish buildings. It's fairly small, and it's really beautiful. . . .

San Miguel Mission, Santa Fe

7 SNAPSHOT

Source: World Tourism Organization

Talk about these questions.

Why do you think France has the most tourists?
Which countries on this list would you most like to visit? Rank the countries from 1 to 10.
Which country did you rank number 1? Why?

8 CONVERSATION *Giving suggestions*

A Listen and practice.

David: Can you tell me a little about Mexico City?
Maria: Sure I can. What would you like to know?
David: Well, what's a good time to visit?
Maria: I think you can go anytime. The weather is always nice.
David: Oh, good! And what should I see there?
Maria: Well, you should visit the National Museum and go to the Palace of Fine Arts.
David: What else?
Maria: Oh, you shouldn't miss the Pyramid of the Sun. It's very interesting.
David: It all sounds really exciting!

CLASS AUDIO ONLY **B** Listen to the rest of the conversation.

1. Where is David from?
2. What should you do there?

9 GRAMMAR FOCUS

Modal verbs can and should

Can you tell me about Mexico?	Yes, I **can**./No, I **can't**.
What **can** you do there?	You **can** see the Palace of Fine Arts.
Should I go to the Palace of Fine Arts?	Yes, you **should**./No, you **shouldn't**.
What **should** I see there?	You **should** visit the National Museum. You **shouldn't** miss the Pyramid of the Sun.

A Complete these sentences about things to do in France. Use the verbs from the list.

1. You .... Paris.
2. You .... the Eiffel Tower.
3. You .... French food.
4. You .... shopping at the flea markets.
5. You .... a boat ride on the Seine River.
6. You .... a morning at the Louvre Museum.

should spend
can see
can go
should visit
should try
shouldn't miss

B ***Pair work*** Write answers to these questions about your country. Then compare with a partner.

1. What time of year should you go there?
2. What are three things you can do there?
3. Can you buy anything special?
4. What shouldn't a visitor miss?
5. What shouldn't people do?

1. You should go in the spring.

10 *PRONUNCIATION* Can't *and* shouldn't

A Listen and practice these sentences. Notice how the *t* in **can't** and **shouldn't** is pronounced.

You can'**t** walk home on the streets late at night.
You shouldn'**t** miss the night markets.
You can'**t** go shopping on Sundays.
You shouldn'**t** swim at the beaches.

B ***Class activity*** Are any of these statements true about your city?

interchange 11
City guide
Make a guide to fun and interesting places in your city. Turn to page IC-15.

11 *LISTENING*

CLASS AUDIO ONLY

A Listen to three speakers talk about Japan, Argentina, and Italy. Complete the chart.

	Capital city	What visitors should see or do
1. Japan		
2. Argentina		
3. Italy		

CLASS AUDIO ONLY

B Listen again. One thing about each country is incorrect. What is it?

12 *ON VACATION*

Group work Has anyone in your group visited an interesting country or place in your country? Find out more about it. Start like this and ask questions like the ones below.

A: I visited Malaysia last summer.
B: Did you enjoy it?
A: Yes, I did.
C: . . .

What's the best time of year to visit?
What's the weather like then?
What should tourists see and do there?
What special foods can you eat?
What's the shopping like?
What things should people buy?
What else can visitors do there?

Kuala Lumpur, Malaysia

a market in Kuala Lumpur

13 READING

FAMOUS CITIES

What cities are famous in your country? Why are they famous?

1.

This beautiful city in northeastern Italy is built on about 120 small islands. The city has no roads. Instead, people use boats to travel along the canals. Flat-bottomed boats called gondolas were once the main means of transportation, but today motorboats are more popular. You should see St. Mark's Square – the center of activity in this city. It has wonderful Renaissance buildings.

Which city:
- ☐ Paris
- ☐ Venice
- ☐ Rome

2.

This American city is the main business and cultural center of the Midwest. It is famous for its music, opera, and theater. It also has excellent museums. When shopping in this city, you can visit a long row of fashionable stores on North Michigan Avenue. This area is called the Magnificent Mile. One of the world's tallest buildings, the John Hancock Center, is also on this avenue.

Which city:
- ☐ New York
- ☐ San Francisco
- ☐ Chicago

3.

Travelers use many words to describe this South American city: beautiful, glamorous, sunny, friendly, and exciting. It is the city of the Carnival, when everyone dances the samba in the streets. Tourists also love to visit its fabulous beaches and mountains. You shouldn't miss the National Park of Tijuca – one of the largest city parks in the world.

Which city:
- ☐ Mexico City
- ☐ Rio de Janeiro
- ☐ Havana

A Read descriptions of the three cities. Check (✓) the correct city to match each description.

B Complete the chart with information about each city. Then compare with a partner.

	Where is this city?	What is special about this city?	What should visitors do there?
1.	....	....	....
2.	....	....	....
3.	....	....	....

C ***Class activity*** Which city would you like to visit? Why?

12 It really works!

1 SNAPSHOT

Source: National Center for Health Statistics

Talk about these questions.

Have you had any of these health problems recently? Which ones?
How many times have you been sick in the past year?
What do you do when you have a headache? a cold? insomnia?

2 CONVERSATION *Health problems*

A Listen and practice.

Joan: Hi, Craig! How are you?
Craig: Not so good. I have a terrible cold.
Joan: Really? That's too bad! You should be at home in bed. It's really important to get a lot of rest.
Craig: Yeah, you're right.
Joan: And have you taken anything for it?
Craig: No, I haven't.
Joan: Well, it's helpful to chop up some garlic and cook it in chicken stock. Then drink a cup every half hour. It really works!
Craig: Ugh!

CLASS AUDIO ONLY

B Listen to advice from two more of Craig's co-workers.

What do they suggest?

3 GRAMMAR FOCUS

Infinitive complements

What should you do for a cold? **It's important** to get a lot of rest.
It's a good idea to take some vitamin C.
It's useful to get some cold medicine.
It's helpful to chop up some garlic and cook it.

A Look at these health problems. Choose several pieces of good advice for each problem.

Problems

1. a sore throat ....
2. a cough ....
3. a backache ....
4. a fever ....
5. a toothache ....
6. a bad headache ....
7. a burn ....
8. the flu ....

Advice

a. take some vitamin C
b. put some ointment on it
c. drink lots of liquids
d. go to bed and rest
e. put a heating pad on it
f. put it under cold water
g. take some aspirin
h. get some medicine from the drugstore
i. see the dentist
j. see the doctor

B ***Group work*** Talk about the problems in part A and give advice. What other advice do you have for each problem?

A: What should you do for a sore throat?
B: It's a good idea to get some medicine from the drugstore.
C: Yes. And it's important to drink lots of liquids.
D: Well, I think it's useful to . . . .

C Write advice for these problems. (You will use this advice in Exercise 4.)

a cold
insomnia
sore eyes
sore muscles
stress

For a cold, it's a good idea to . . . .

4 PRONUNCIATION *Reduced form of* to

A Listen and practice. In conversation, **to** is usually reduced to /tə/.

A: What should you do for a fever?
B: It's important **to** take some aspirin.
And it's a good idea **to** see the doctor.

B ***Pair work*** Now look back at part C of Exercise 3. Ask for and give advice about the health problems you wrote about. Pay attention to the pronunciation of **to**.

interchange 12

Talk radio

Imagine you are a talk show host. Give advice to some callers. Turn to page IC-16.

5 WHAT DID YOU DO?

A ***Pair work*** Take turns talking about these problems.

a stomachache an insect bite a sore throat the hiccups

A: Have you ever had a stomachache?
B: Sure I have. Just last night, actually.
A: What did you do?
B: I took some antacid.

B ***Group work*** Compare with other pairs. Tell what you did for each problem.

6 WORD POWER *Containers and medicines*

A Use the words in the list to complete these expressions. Then compare with a partner.

bottle box can package tube

1. a .... of ointment
2. a .... of aspirin
3. a .... of bandages
4. a .... of foot spray
5. a .... of tissues

B What is one more thing you can buy in each of the containers above?

C What common items do you have in your medicine cabinet?

7 CONVERSATION *Giving suggestions*

A Listen and practice.

Pharmacist: Hi. Can I help you?
Mrs. Webb: Yes, please. Could I have something for a cough? I think I'm getting a cold.
Pharmacist: Well, I suggest a box of these cough drops. And you should get a bottle of vitamin C, too.
Mrs. Webb: Thank you. And what do you have for dry skin?
Pharmacist: Try some of this new lotion. It's very good.
Mrs. Webb: OK. Thanks a lot.

CLASS AUDIO ONLY

B Listen to the pharmacist talk to the next customer.

What does the customer want?

8 GRAMMAR FOCUS

Modal verbs *can, could, may* for requests; suggestions

Can/May I help you?	What do you have/suggest for dry skin?
Can I have a box of cough drops?	Try some of this lotion.
Could I have something for a sore throat?	I suggest some ointment.
May I have a bottle of aspirin?	You should get some skin cream.

Complete these conversations with the verbs *can, could, may, have, suggest, try,* or *should.* Then compare and practice with a partner.

1. A: .... I help you?
   B: Yes. .... I have something for tired eyes?
   A: Sure. I .... a bottle of eye drops.

2. A: What do you .... for sore muscles?
   B: You .... try a tube of this ointment. It's excellent.
   A: OK. I'll take it.

3. A: .... I have a box of cold tablets, please?
   B: Here you are.
   A: And what do you .... for insomnia?
   B: .... some of these sleeping pills.
   A: OK. Thanks.

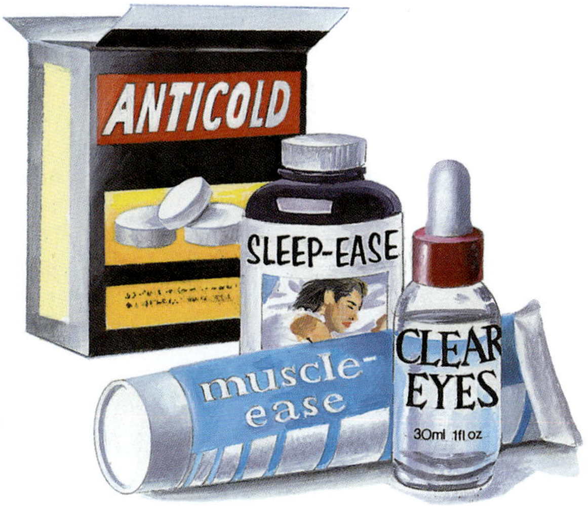

9 LISTENING

CLASS AUDIO ONLY

Listen to people talking about things in a drugstore. Check (✓) the items they buy.

1. ☐ ☐

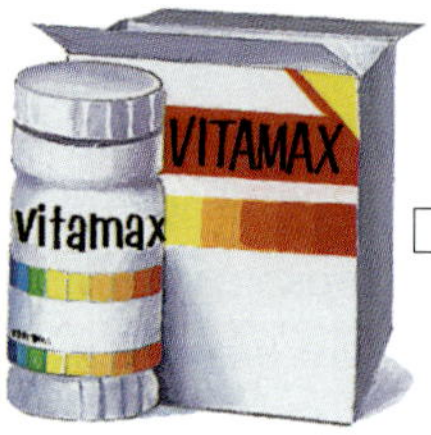

2. ☐ ☐

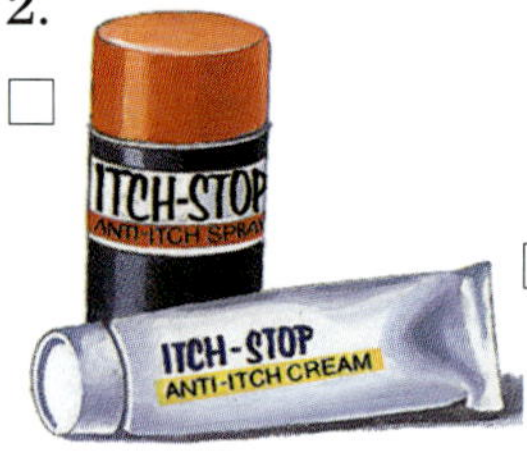

3. ☐ ☐

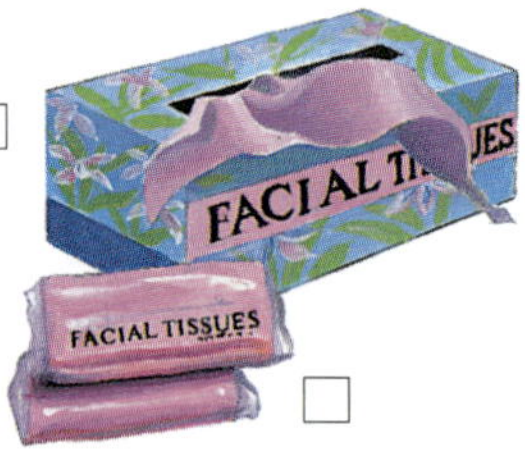

4. ☐ ☐

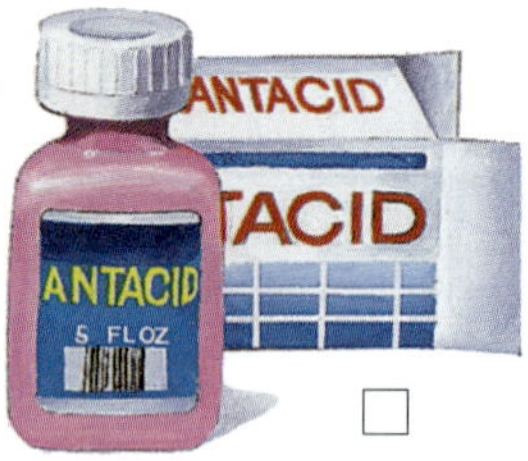

10 ROLE PLAY *Can I help you?*

Student A: You are a customer in a drugstore. You need:

something for a sunburn
something for sore muscles
something for a sore throat

Ask for some suggestions.

Student B: You are a pharmacist in a drugstore. A customer needs some things. Make some suggestions.

a can of sunburn spray

a tube of muscle ointment

a bottle of throat spray

Change roles and try the role play again. Make up your own information.

11 WRITING

A Write about an interesting home or folk remedy.

I have a good home remedy for a sore throat. I learned about it from my grandmother. Cut slices of meat, put pepper on them, and then tie them around your throat with a cloth. It's also a good idea to go to bed and rest. This always works (my grandmother says!).

B ***Pair work*** Take turns reading your compositions. Which home remedy is the most interesting?

12 READING

Grandma knows best!

When you have a minor health problem, do you usually go to the doctor, get something from the drugstore, or use a home remedy?

When people have a cold, a fever, or the flu, they usually go to the doctor for help, or they get some medicine from the drugstore. But many people also use home remedies for common illnesses. Here are some simple home remedies.

Bee stings and insect bites

Wash the sting or bite. Put some meat tenderizer on a handkerchief and then put the handkerchief on the bite for half an hour. To avoid insect bites, it's helpful to eat garlic or take garlic pills.

Burns

Put the burn under cold water or put a cold handkerchief on it. It's important not to put ice on the burn.

Colds

Lots of people eat hot chicken soup when they have a cold. They find it clears the head and the nose. Some people rub oil on their chest for a cold. Other people drink a mixture of red pepper, hot water, sugar, lemon juice, and milk or vinegar.

Cough

Drink warm liquids or take some honey.

Headaches

Apply an ice pack or cold cloth to your head, or splash your face with cold water. It's also a good idea to put your hands into hot water and leave them there for several minutes. Also, you shouldn't read or watch TV.

Insomnia

Drink a large glass of warm milk. It's also a good idea to soak in a warm bath.

A ***Pair work*** Read the article. Then cover the article and complete the chart. What problems are these things good for?

Advice	Problem
1. hot chicken soup / rubbing oil on your chest	....
2. a warm bath / warm milk	....
3. garlic / meat tenderizer	....
4. an ice pack / putting your hands in hot water	....
5. cold water / cold handkerchief	....
6. honey / warm liquids	....

B ***Group work*** Do you use any of these remedies? What other home remedies do you use?

Review of Units 9–12

1 WHAT WAS IT LIKE?

Group work Ask these questions around the group.

Have you ever . . . ?

been on a camping trip
gotten a famous person's autograph
given first aid to someone
been on a blind date
lost your credit cards
gone windsurfing
been in an accident
had food poisoning
kept a diary
fainted

When someone answers "Yes," he or she explains what happened, and the other students ask for more information.

A: **Have you ever** gone windsurfing?
B: Yeah, I have. I tried it last year in Hawaii. It was really fun!
C: **What was it like?** Was it difficult?
B: Yes, it was at first. Has anyone else ever gone windsurfing?
D: . . .

2 ROLE PLAY Missing person

Student A: You are visiting an amusement park with your English class. One of your classmates is lost. You are talking to a security officer. Answer the officer's questions and describe one of your classmates. (Don't give the student's name.)

Student B: You are a security officer at an amusement park. Someone is talking to you about a lost classmate. Ask questions to complete the form. Then look around the class. Can you find the lost student?

Change roles and try the role play again.

MISSING PERSONS REPORT

Name	
Age	
Height	
Hair	
Eyes	
Clothing	

3 WHICH ONE IS BILL?

Pair work Look at this picture of a party. Write sentences identifying each person.

Bill is the man in the black shirt./Bill is the one sitting next to Louisa.

4 LISTENING

CLASS AUDIO ONLY

Listen to Jenny talking about Honolulu. What does she say about these things? Complete the chart.

What she says about	
1. size	....
2. weather	....
3. prices	....
4. a famous place	....

5 DIFFICULT SITUATIONS

A ***Group work*** What do you do in these situations? Discuss each situation using expressions from the box. Write down your ideas.

What do you do when . . . ?

1. you have an argument with a friend
2. it's 2:00 A.M. and you can't sleep
3. you feel very stressed
4. you can't remember someone's name
5. you need to study, but you can't concentrate

useful expressions

It's useful to . . . .
It's helpful to . . . .
It's a good idea to . . . .
You can . . . .
You should . . . .

1. It's a good idea to apologize right away.

B ***Class activity*** Read your group's ideas to the class.

13 May I take your order, please?

1 SNAPSHOT

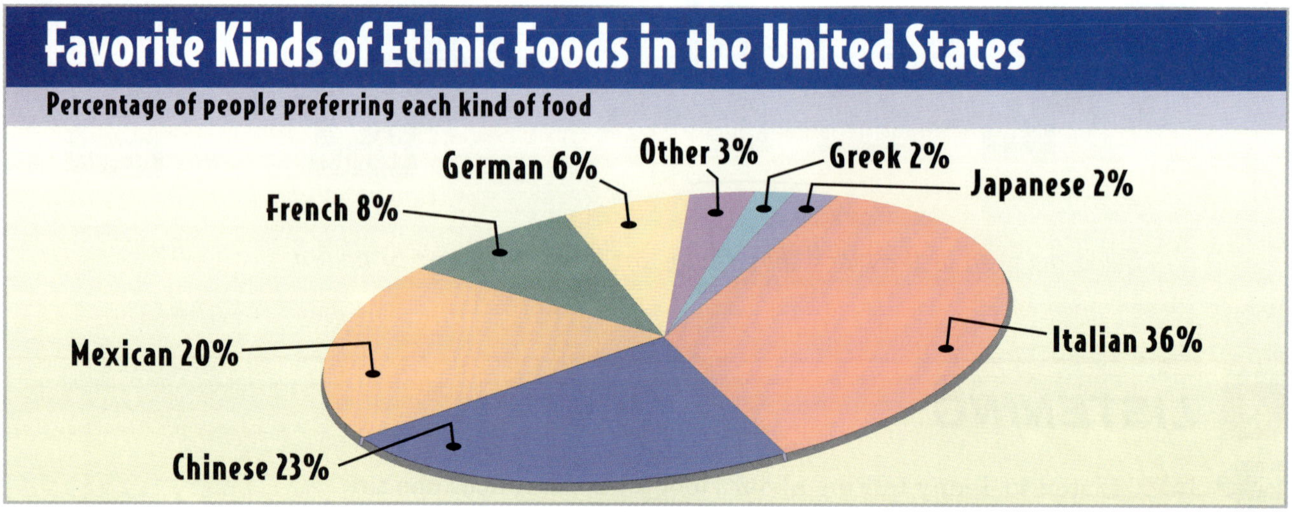

Source: National Restaurant Association

Talk about these questions.

Are there restaurants in your city that serve these kinds of foods?
Which of the foods have you tried? Which would you like to try?
What other kinds of foods do you like?

2 CONVERSATION *Going out for dinner*

A Listen and practice.

Sandy: Say, do you want to go out to dinner tonight?
Bob: Sure. Where would you like to go?
Sandy: Well, what do you think of Indian food?
Bob: I love it, but I'm not really in the mood for it today.
Sandy: Yeah. I'm not either, I guess. It's a bit spicy.
Bob: Hmm. How do you like Japanese food?
Sandy: Oh, I like it a lot.
Bob: I do, too. And I know a nice Japanese restaurant near here – it's called Iroha.
Sandy: Oh, I've always wanted to go there.
Bob: Terrific! Let's go!

CLASS AUDIO ONLY

B Listen to the rest of the conversation.

1. What time do they decide to have dinner? Why?
2. Where do they decide to meet?

3 GRAMMAR FOCUS

So, too, neither, either

I like Japanese food a lot.
So do I. / I do, **too**.
Really? I don't like it very much.

I'm crazy about dessert.
So am I. / I am, **too**.
Oh, I'm not at all.

I can eat really spicy food.
So can I. / I can, **too**.
Oh, I can't.

I don't like greasy food.
Neither do I. / I don't **either**.
Oh, I like it a lot.

I'm not in the mood for Indian food.
Neither am I. / I'm not **either**.
Really? I am.

I can't stand fast food.
Neither can I. / I can't **either**.
Oh, I love it!

healthy greasy salty rich spicy delicious bland

A Write responses to show agreement with these statements. Then compare with a partner.

1. I'm not crazy about French food. ....
2. I can eat any kind of food. ....
3. I think Mexican food is delicious. ....
4. I can't stand greasy food. ....
5. I don't like salty food. ....
6. I'm in the mood for something spicy. ....
7. I'm crazy about Korean food. ....
8. I don't enjoy rich food very much. ....
9. I always eat healthy food. ....
10. I can't eat bland food. ....

B ***Pair work*** Take turns responding to the statements in part A again. Give your own opinion when responding.

C Write statements about these things. (You will use the statements in Exercise 4.)

1. two kinds of food you like
2. two kinds of food you can't stand
3. two kinds of food you are in the mood for

4 PRONUNCIATION *Stress in responses*

A Listen and practice. The last word of each response is usually stressed.

So do **Í**.	I do, **tóo**.	Neither am **Í**.	I'm not **éither**.
Neither do **Í**.	I don't **éither**.	So can **Í**.	I can, **tóo**.
So am **Í**.	I am, **tóo**.	Neither can **Í**.	I can't **éither**.

B ***Pair work*** Take turns reading the statements you wrote in part C of Exercise 3. Pay attention to the stress in your responses.

A: I don't really like greasy food.
B: I don't **éither**. (Neither do **Í**.) It's not very healthy.

5 WORD POWER *Restaurant orders*

A ***Pair work*** Complete the chart with words from the list. Then add two more words to each category. What's your favorite food in each category?

apple pie	cold pasta salad	chicken broth	chocolate cake	coffee
cole slaw	onion soup	grilled salmon	hamburger & fries	ice cream
iced tea	milk	mixed greens	roast turkey	clam chowder

Soups	Salads	Main dishes	Desserts	Beverages
....	....	....	....	....
....	....	....	....	....
....	....	....	....	....
....	....	....	....	....
....	....	....	....	....

B What foods do you think these people like best? Use items from the chart above or your own ideas.

1. ....

2. ....

3. ....

4. ....

CLASS AUDIO ONLY

C Listen to each of the people above talking about their favorite foods and take notes. How similar were your guesses?

6 CONVERSATION *Ordering a meal*

Listen and practice.

Waiter: May I take your order?
Customer: Yes. I'd like a hamburger and a large order of french fries, please.
Waiter: All right. And would you like a salad?
Customer: Yes, I'll have a mixed green salad.
Waiter: OK. What kind of dressing would you like? We have vinaigrette, Italian, and French.
Customer: Italian, please.
Waiter: And would you like anything to drink?
Customer: Yes, I'd like a large soda, please.

7 GRAMMAR FOCUS

Modal verbs would *and* will *for requests*

What **would** you **like** to eat?	**I'd like** a hamburger. **I'll have** a small salad.	***Contractions*** I will = **I'll** I would = **I'd**
What kind of dressing **would** you like?	**I'd like** Italian, please. **I'll have** French.	
What **would** you **like** to drink?	**I'd like** a large soda. **I'll have** coffee.	
Would you **like** anything else?	Yes, please. **I'd like** some water. No, thank you. That **will be** all.	

Complete this conversation. Then practice with a partner.

Waitress: What .... you like to order?
Customer: I .... have the fried chicken.
Waitress: .... you like rice or potatoes?
Customer: Potatoes, please.
Waitress: What kind of potatoes would you .... ? Mashed, baked, or french fries?
Customer: I .... like french fries.
Waitress: OK. And what will you .... to drink?
Customer: I guess I .... have a cup of coffee.
Waitress: Would you .... anything else?
Customer: No, that .... be all for now, thanks.

Later

Waitress: Would you .... dessert?
Customer: Yes, I .... like ice cream.
Waitress: What flavor .... you like?
Customer: Hmm. I .... have chocolate, please.
Waitress: OK. I'll bring it right away.

8 ROLE PLAY *In a coffee shop*

Student A: You are a customer in a coffee shop.
This is what you want to order for lunch:

tomato and cucumber salad	garlic bread
spaghetti and meatballs	iced tea with lemon

Student B: You are the waiter or waitress.
Take your customer's order.

Change roles and try the role play again. Make up your own information.

9 LISTENING

CLASS AUDIO ONLY **A** Listen to Tom and Tina ordering in a restaurant. What did each of them order? Fill in their orders.

CLASS AUDIO ONLY **B** Listen to the rest of the conversation. What happened?

10 WRITING *Restaurant reviews*

A Have you eaten out at a restaurant recently? How was it? Write a review of the restaurant and the meal you had there.

The Surf and Turf Restaurant

I had lunch at the Surf and Turf Restaurant last week. It's a steak and seafood restaurant. I ordered a steak and a Caesar salad. For dessert, I had chocolate cake and coffee. My meal cost about $24 with the tip.

The waiter was helpful. The coffee wasn't very good, but the salad and steak were delicious. I'd go back to the Surf and Turf.

B ***Group work*** Take turns reading your reviews to the group. Is there a restaurant you would like to try?

interchange 13

Are you ready to order?

Have lunch at The Corner Cafe. Student A turns to page IC-17. Students B and C turn to page IC-18.

... or Not to Tip?

Do you tip for services in your country? When?

Canadians and Americans usually tip in places like restaurants, airports, hotels, and hair salons because many people who work in these places get low salaries. A tip shows that the customer is pleased with the service.

At airports, porters usually get a dollar tip for each bag. Hotel bellhops usually get a dollar for carrying one or two suitcases. A hotel door attendant or parking valet also gets about a dollar for getting a taxi or for parking a car. Many people also tip hotel room attendants, especially when they stay in a hotel for several days. They usually leave a dollar for each day.

The usual tip for other kinds of services – for example, for taxi drivers, barbers, hairdressers, waiters, and waitresses – is between 10 and 20 percent of the bill. The size of the tip depends on how pleased the customer is. In most restaurants, the check does not include a service charge. If the group is large, however, there may be an added service charge. There is no tipping in cafeterias or fast-food restaurants.

A ***Pair work*** Read the article. Then talk about these questions.

1. How much should you tip someone in North America who:

   takes your bag at an airport?
   parks your car at a hotel or restaurant?
   serves you in a fast-food restaurant?

2. What tip should you leave for the following:

   a $27 haircut?
   a $50 restaurant check?
   a $14 taxi fare?

B ***Group work*** Do you think tipping is a good or bad custom? Why?

14 The biggest and the best!

1 WORD POWER *Geography*

A Circle the word that doesn't belong in each list. Then compare with a partner.

1.	2.	3.	4.
canyon	lake	hill	desert
cliff	plateau	mountain	forest
swamp	river	volcano	plains
valley	sea	ocean	waterfall

B Find examples of some of the words above in this picture. What other geography words can you think of?

C Add two names to these lists. Then compare with a partner.

Mountains	Rivers	Continents	Oceans
Mount Everest	*the Amazon River*	*Africa*	*the Pacific Ocean*

2 CONVERSATION Describing countries

Listen and practice.

the Great Barrier Reef

Paul: I'm going to Australia next year. Aren't you from "down under," Kelly?
Kelly: That's right.
Paul: I hear there's not much pollution, and the beaches are clean and beautiful.
Kelly: Oh, yes. Australia has some of the most famous beaches in the world – like Bondi Beach.
Paul: What else should I see?
Kelly: Well, the Great Barrier Reef is there. It's the longest coral reef in the world.
Paul: Wow! It sounds beautiful. You're lucky to be an Australian.
Kelly: Thanks, but actually, I'm a New Zealander.

3 GRAMMAR FOCUS

Comparisons with adjectives

Adjective	*Comparative*	*Superlative*
large	larger	the largest
long	longer	the longest
dry	drier	the driest
big	bigger	the biggest
beautiful	more beautiful	the most beautiful
famous	more famous	the most famous
good	better	the best
bad	worse	the worst

Which country is **larger**, Canada or China?
Canada is **larger than** China.

Which country is **the largest**: Russia, Canada, or China?
Russia is **the largest** country of the three.

What is **the most beautiful** mountain in the world?
I think Fujiyama is **the most beautiful**.

For more information on comparatives and superlatives, see the appendix at the back of the book.

A Complete questions 1 to 4 with comparatives. Complete questions 5 to 8 with superlatives. Then ask and answer the questions. Check your answers in the appendix.

1. Which country is .... , Monaco or Vatican City? (small)
2. Which waterfall is .... , Niagara Falls or Angel Falls? (high)
3. Which city is .... , Hong Kong or Cairo? (crowded)
4. Which lake is .... , the Caspian Sea or Lake Superior? (large)
5. Which mountain is .... : Mount McKinley, Mount Everest, or Fujiyama? (tall)
6. What is .... river in the world, the Nile or the Amazon? (long)
7. Which country is .... with tourists: Spain, France, or Italy? (popular)
8. What is .... ocean in the world, the Pacific or the Atlantic? (deep)

B ***Class activity*** Write four questions like those in part A about your country or other countries. Then ask your questions around the class.

4 PRONUNCIATION *Questions of choice*

Listen to the intonation of questions where there is a choice. Then practice the questions.

Which country is bigger, China or Russia?

Which is the largest desert in the world, the Australian or the Sahara?

Which country is the most interesting: Korea, Brazil, or France?

5 IN YOUR OPINION

Group work Answer these questions about your country. Be ready to explain your answers. Then compare in a group.

What are the three most interesting places in your country?
What's the best time of year to visit?
What are the most famous tourist attractions?
What's the most beautiful place in your country?

interchange 14

How much do you know?

You probably know more than you think you do! Take a quiz. Turn to page IC-19.

6 WRITING

A Write about one of the places or things you discussed in Exercise 5.

I think the most beautiful place in my country is a town called Ubud on Bali. It's located in the mountains, and there are lots of rice fields. Many artists live and work there. . . .

B ***Pair work*** Exchange papers and read each other's compositions.

Ubud, Bali, Indonesia

7 LISTENING *TV game show*

CLASS AUDIO ONLY

Three people are playing a TV game show. Listen to each question, and check (✓) the correct answer.

1. ☑ the Statue of Liberty
   ☐ the Eiffel Tower
   ☐ the Empire State Building

2. ☐ Concorde
   ☑ 747
   ☐ DC-10

3. ☐ gold
   ☐ butter
   ☐ feathers

4. ☐ the U.S.
   ☐ China
   ☑ Canada

5. ☐ Moscow
   ☑ New York
   ☐ Shanghai

6. ☐ Australia
   ☑ Argentina
   ☐ Brazil

8 SNAPSHOT

Source: Council on Tall Buildings and Urban Habitats

Talk about these questions.

Would you like to visit any of these places? Which ones? Why?
Can you identify these buildings in your city?
The tallest building: ....
The oldest building: ....
The most beautiful building: ....

9 CONVERSATION *Distance and measurements*

A Listen and practice.

Paul: So, what's New Zealand like?
Kelly: Oh, it's beautiful. It has lots of farms, and it's very mountainous.
Paul: Mountainous? Really? I didn't know that. How high are the mountains?
Kelly: Well, the highest one is Mount Cook. It's about 3,800 meters high.
Paul: Hmm. How far is New Zealand from Australia?
Kelly: Well, I live in Auckland, and Auckland is about 2,000 kilometers from Sydney.
Paul: Well, maybe I should visit you next year, too.
Kelly: That would be great!

Auckland, "the City of Sails"

CLASS AUDIO ONLY **B** Listen to the rest of the conversation.

What are some things New Zealand is famous for?

10 GRAMMAR FOCUS

Questions with *how*

How far is New Zealand from Australia?	It's about 2,000 kilometers.	(1,200 miles)
How big is Singapore?	It's 620 square kilometers.	(239 square miles)
How high is Mount Everest?	It's 8,848 meters **high.**	(29,028 feet)
How deep is the Grand Canyon?	It's about 1,900 meters **deep.**	(6,250 feet)
How long is the Mississippi River?	It's about 6,019 kilometers **long.**	(3,740 miles)
How hot is New Zealand in the summer?	It gets up to about 23° Celsius.	(74° Fahrenheit)
How cold is it in the winter?	It goes down to about 10° Celsius.	(50° Fahrenheit)

A Write the questions to these answers. Then practice with a partner.

1. A: How tall is Angel Falls. ?
   B: Angel Falls is 979 meters (3,212 feet) high.
2. A: How big is Ca? ?
   B: California is about 411,000 square kilometers (159,000 square miles).
3. A: How long ?
   B: The Nile is 6,670 kilometers (4,145 miles) long.
4. A: How Hot is Wash. D.C. in the Summer ?
   B: Washington, D.C., gets up to about 32° Celsius (90° Fahrenheit) in the summer.

B ***Group work*** Think of five questions with *how* about places in your country or other countries you know. Ask and answer your questions in groups.

"How cold is Seoul in the winter?"

11 READING

Things You Can Do to Help the Environment

Is pollution in your country: ■ serious? ■ under control? ■ increasing? ■ decreasing?

Our environment is in trouble. People and industries are polluting the air, rivers, lakes, and seas. You may think that there's nothing you can do to help. That's not true. In fact, there are many things you can do to help the environment. Here are a few.

Cars

The burning of gasoline is one of the biggest sources of carbon monoxide (CO) in the atmosphere. Some people believe that CO is causing global warming. They think CO thins the ozone layer, which protects us from the sun's rays. So try to walk, bicycle, or use public transportation. And if you drive a car, drive at a steady speed – this is more efficient than speeding up and slowing down.

Products

Don't use disposable products. In a single year, people in the United States use enough disposable diapers to reach to the moon and back seven times. If you use disposable products, use products made from recycled materials. Also, recycle whenever possible. Recycling one aluminum can saves enough energy to run a TV for three hours.

Energy

The biggest use of home energy is for heating and cooling homes. So turn the heat down, especially at night. Replace regular light bulbs with fluorescent or halogen bulbs, which use less energy.

Water

Showers use a lot of water. In one week a typical American family uses as much water as a person drinks in three years! Buying a special "low-flow" shower head or taking shorter showers can cut this use in half. Also, fix any leaky faucets.

A ***Pair work*** Read the article. Then talk about these questions.

1. Which of the advice above is new to you?
2. Do you follow any of the advice in the article?
3. Which are the three best pieces of advice?
4. What are two other things people can do to protect the environment?

B ***Group work*** Look at the photos in the article. Which ones show environmental problems? Which show solutions? Describe what is right or wrong in each photo.

15 I'm going to see a musical.

1 SNAPSHOT

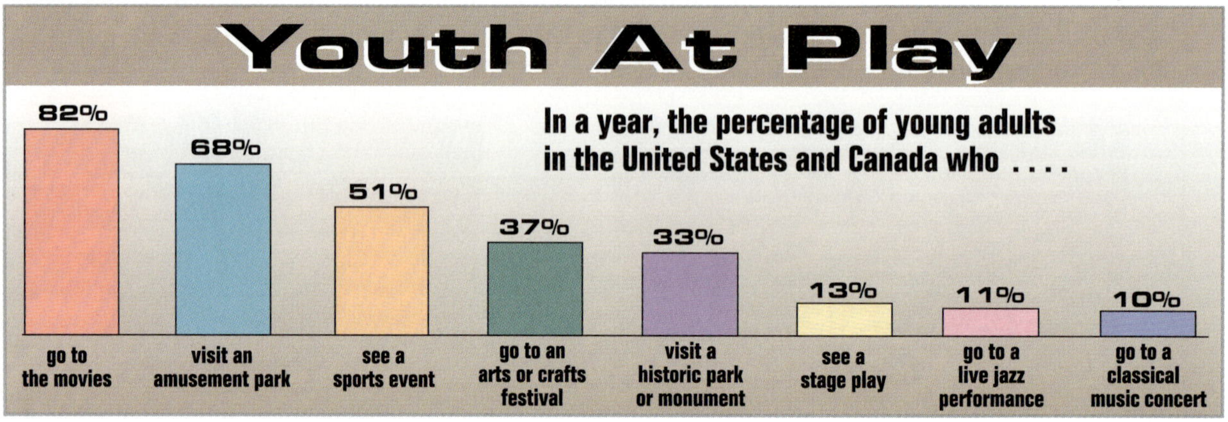

Source: National Endowment for the Arts

Talk about these questions.

Which of these activities have you done in the past year?
Which of these activities would you like to do?
What other activities do you like to do?

2 CONVERSATION *Talking about plans*

A Listen and practice.

Tony: Say, Anna, what are you doing tonight? Would you like to go out?
Anna: Oh, sorry, I can't. I'm going to work late tonight. I have to finish this report.
Tony: Well, how about tomorrow night? Are you doing anything then?
Anna: No, I'm not. What are you planning to do?
Tony: I'm going to see a musical. Would you like to come?
Anna: Sure, I'd love to! But let *me* pay for the tickets this time. It's my turn.
Tony: All right! Thanks!

CLASS AUDIO ONLY **B** Listen to the rest of the conversation.

1. What musical are they going to see?
2. What are they doing before the musical?
3. Where are they going to meet?
4. What time are they meeting?

3 GRAMMAR FOCUS

Future with present continuous and be going to

With present continuous	*With* be going to *+ verb*	*Time expressions*
What **are** you **doing** tonight? **I'm going** to a movie.	What **is** she **going to do** tonight? She**'s going to work** late.	tonight tomorrow on Friday
Are you **doing** anything tomorrow night? No, I'm not.	**Are** they **going to see** a musical tomorrow night? Yes, they are.	this weekend next week

A Complete the invitations in column A with the present continuous used as future. Complete the responses in column B with *be going to.*

A

1. What .... you .... (do) tomorrow? Would you like to go out?
2. .... you .... (do) anything on Saturday night? Do you want to see a movie?
3. We .... (have) friends over for a barbecue on Sunday. Would you and your parents like to come?

B

a. Well, my father .... (visit) my brother at college. But my mother and I .... (be) home. We'd love to come!

b. Sorry, I can't. I .... (work) overtime. How about Saturday?

c. Can we go to a late show? I .... (stay) at the office till 7:00. After that I .... (go) to the gym.

B Match the invitations in column A with the responses in column B. Then practice with a partner.

4 WORD POWER *Leisure activities*

A Complete the word map with activities from the list. Then add two more words to each category.

art show
barbecue
baseball game
beach party
car show
comedy act
craft fair
hockey game
picnic
play
rock concert
tennis tournament

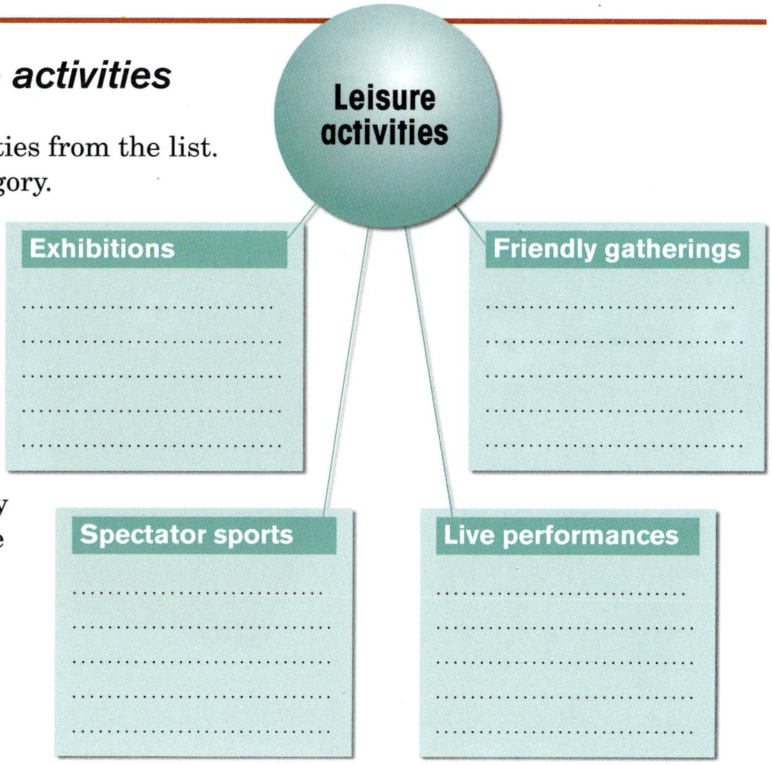

B ***Pair work*** Are you going to do any of the activities on the chart? When are you doing them? Talk with a partner.

A: I'm going to see a rock concert.
B: Really? When?
A: On Friday.
B: . . .

5 ROLE PLAY *An invitation*

Student A: Choose an activity from Exercise 4 and invite a partner to go with you. Be ready to say where and when the activity is.

A: Say, are you doing anything on . . . ?
Would you like to . . . ?

Student B: Your partner invites you out. Either accept the invitation and ask for more information, or say you can't go and give an excuse.

Accept	*Refuse*
B: That sounds interesting. Where is it?	B: Oh, I'm sorry, but I can't go. I'm . . . .

Change roles and try the role play again.

interchange 15

What are you going to do?

Find out what your classmates are doing over the weekend. Turn to page IC-20.

6 CONVERSATION *Telephone messages*

Listen and practice.

Secretary: Good morning, Parker Industries.
Mr. Kale: Hello. May I speak to Ms. Graham, please?
Secretary: I'm sorry. She's not in. Can I take a message?
Mr. Kale: Yes, please. This is Mr. Kale.
Secretary: Is that G-A-L-E?
Mr. Kale: No, it's K-A-L-E.
Secretary: All right.
Mr. Kale: Please tell her our meeting is on Friday at 2:30.
Secretary: Friday at 2:30.
Mr. Kale: And would you ask her to call me this afternoon? My number is 356-4031.
Secretary: 356-4031. Yes, Mr. Kale. I'll give Ms. Graham the message.
Mr. Kale: Thank you. Good-bye.
Secretary: Good-bye.

To: *Ms. Graham*
Date: *August 10* Time: ______

WHILE YOU WERE OUT

From: *Mr. Kale*
of: ______
Phone: *356-4031* ext: ______
Message: ______
The meeting is on Friday at 2:30.
Please call him this afternoon.
Taken by: ______

7 GRAMMAR FOCUS

Tell *and* ask

Statement	*Messages with a statement*
The meeting is on Friday.	**Please tell Ann (that)** the meeting is on Friday. **Would you tell her (that) . . . ?** **Could you tell her (that) . . . ?**
Request	***Messages with a request***
Call me this afternoon.	**Please ask him to** call me this afternoon. **Would you ask him to . . . ?** **Could you tell him to . . . ?**

Look at the message slips. Ask someone to pass on these messages. Use the words in parentheses. Then compare with a partner.

1. *Kim – The movie is at 7:00 tonight.*
   (could) *Could you tell Kim the movie is at 7:00?*
2. *Mike – Pick me up at home around 4:00.*
   (would)
3. *Maria – The concert on Saturday is canceled.*
   (please)
4. *Jim – Bring the tickets for the hockey game tonight.*
   (could)
5. *Ann – The museum opens at 10:00 tomorrow morning.*
   (would)
6. *Alex – Meet us in front of the cafeteria at 12:15.*
   (please)

8 WRITING

Pair work You want to give messages to people in your class. Write a request to your partner. Ask him or her to give the messages for you.

Dear Su Hee,
I'm not going to be in class tomorrow. Would you please ask Ms. King to save any handouts for me? Also, could you tell Steve that I can't meet him for dinner after class?
Thanks,
Juan

9 PRONUNCIATION *Reduced forms of* could you *and* would you

A Listen and practice. Notice how **could you** and **would you** are reduced in conversation.

/cʊdʒə/
Could you tell Matt the meeting is at 5:00?

/wʊdʒə/
Would you ask him to pick me up at 4:30?

B Practice these questions with reduced forms.

Could you ask her to return my dictionary?
Would you tell him there's a picnic tomorrow?

10 LISTENING *Take a message*

CLASS AUDIO ONLY

Listen to telephone calls to Mr. Kim and Ms. Carson, and write down the messages.

1.

To: Mr. ________
Date: ________ Time: ________

WHILE YOU WERE OUT

From: ________
of: City ________
Phone: ________ ext: ________
Message: ________
Call Mrs. ________
____
Taken by: ________

2.

To: Wendy ________
Date: ________ Time: ________

WHILE YOU WERE OUT

From: ________
of: ____ National ________
Phone: ________ ext: ________
Message: ________
____
____
Taken by: ________

11 ROLE PLAY *Who's calling?*

Student A: Call your friend David to tell him this:

There's a party at Bob's house on Saturday night.
Bob's address is 414 Maple St., Apt. 202.
Pick me up at 8:00 P.M.

Student B: Someone calls for your brother David. He isn't in. Take a message for him.

Change roles and try another role play.

Student A: Someone calls for your sister Carol. She isn't in. Take a message for her.

Student B: Call your friend Carol to tell her this:

There's no class next Friday afternoon.
The class is going to a movie at Westwood Theater.
Meet us in front of the theater at 4:30.

useful expressions

May I speak to . . . ?
Can I take a message?
I'll give . . . the message.

12 READING

Ways to Keep Phone Calls Short

Do you like to talk on the phone?
Do you think that you spend too much time on the phone?

The phone rings. It's a friend who wants to tell you about his or her latest health problem. You hate to be rude and cut your friend off, but what can you do? Time management consultant Stephanie Winston, author of *Stephanie Winston's Best Organizing Tips,* offers this advice:

1. **Don't ask questions like "What's new?"** They give the impression that you have time to chat. After "hello," get right to the heart of the matter.
2. **Time *your* calls intelligently.** If you make a call right before lunch or dinner, or at the end of the workday, people chat less.
3. **Set a time limit.** Start with, "Hi, I've only got a few minutes, but I wanted to talk to you about . . ." Or, "Gee, I'd love to talk more, but I only have a couple of minutes before I have to run errands."
4. **Jump on a pause.** Even the most talkative caller has to pause now and then. Quickly say, "It has been great talking with you." Then end the conversation.
5. **Forget niceties.** Some people just don't take a hint. Interrupt your caller and say, "I'd like to talk to you longer, but I'm pressed for time. Good-bye." Then hang up. Don't ask for permission to end the conversation.
6. **Find a "partner in crime."** If nothing else works, ask someone in your home to help you. For example, one woman signals her husband, who yells, "Jane, I think the roast is burning!"
7. **Avoid the phone completely.** Use an answering machine to screen calls. If you have an important message for a chatterbox, leave the message when he or she isn't in.

A Read the article. Then look at these sentences. Check (✓) the things you can say to keep phone calls short.

- ☐ 1. I'm glad you feel better. What can I do for you?
- ☐ 2. I have to go now. Good-bye.
- ☐ 3. Hi. How are things?
- ☐ 4. I need to get off the phone now. There's someone at the door.
- ☐ 5. So, what else is new?
- ☐ 6. No, I'm not busy right now.
- ☐ 7. I'm sorry to call you at dinnertime, but I have just one question.
- ☐ 8. I only have three minutes before I have to leave.

B ***Pair work*** Talk about these questions.

1. Which advice have you used sometimes?
2. Which do you think are the three best pieces of advice?
3. What else can you do to keep phone calls short?

16 A change for the better!

1 SNAPSHOT

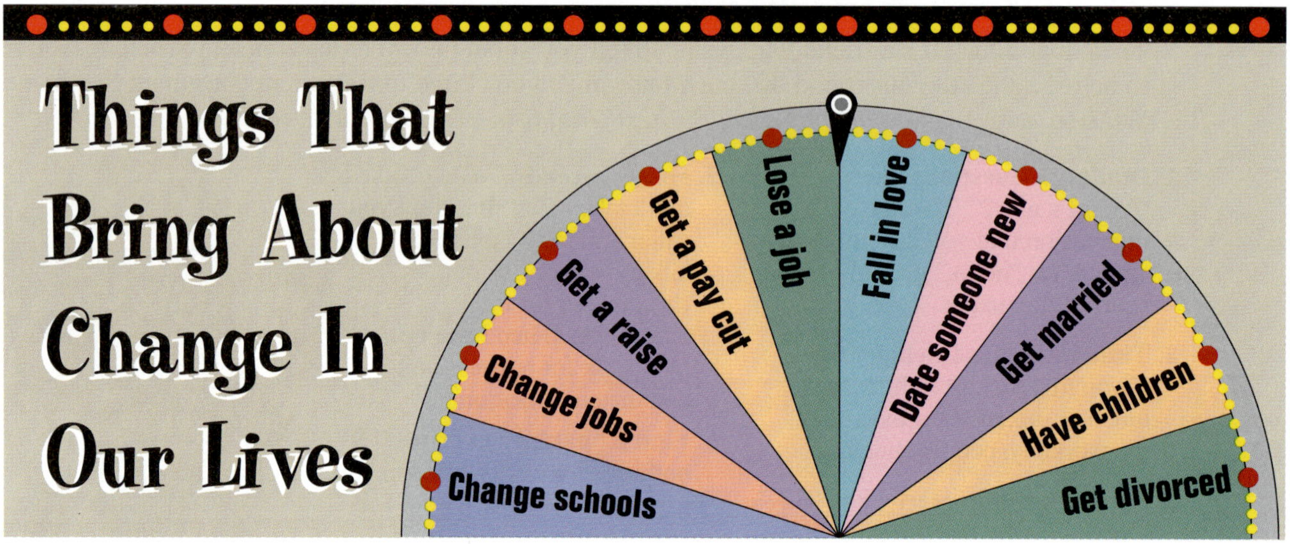

Talk about these questions.

Have any of these things happened to you in the last few years?
How have they changed you?
What other things bring about change in our lives?

2 CONVERSATION Catching up

A Listen and practice.

Brian: Diane Grant? I haven't seen you for ages.
Diane: Brian! How have you been?
Brian: Pretty good. Say, you've really changed!
Diane: Oh, well, I've lost some weight. And my hair is longer than before.
Brian: Well, you look great! How are you?
Diane: I'm doing really well. I got married about three years ago. I have two kids now.
Brian: That's terrific!

CLASS AUDIO ONLY

B Listen to the rest of the conversation.

How has Brian changed?

3 GRAMMAR FOCUS

Describing changes

With the present tense	With the comparative	With the past tense	With the present perfect
I **have** two kids now.	My job is **more stressful** (now).	I **got** married.	I**'ve lost** weight.
I **don't smoke** anymore.	My hair is **longer** (**than** before).	I **moved** to a new city.	I**'ve grown** a mustache.

A How have you changed in the last five years? Check (✓) the statements that are true for you. If a statement isn't true, give the correct information.

☐ 1. I've changed my hairstyle.
☐ 2. I dress differently now.
☐ 3. I've lost weight.
☐ 4. I moved into my own apartment.
☐ 5. I got married.
☐ 6. I'm more outgoing than before.
☐ 7. I don't go to many parties anymore.
☐ 8. My life is easier now.

B ***Pair work*** Compare your responses in part A. Have you changed in similar ways?

C ***Group work*** Write five sentences describing other changes in your life. Then compare in groups. Who in the group has changed the most?

4 LISTENING *Memory lane*

CLASS AUDIO ONLY

Linda and Scott are looking through a photo album. Listen to their conversation. How have they changed? Write down three changes.

Changes
....
....
....

5 WORD POWER *Things that change*

A Complete the word map with the phrases from the list. Then add two more examples to each category.

cut my hair short
do aerobics
eat more vegetables
get dressed up
get up early
grow a beard
learn to swim
learn to type
quit smoking
speak English
start cooking
wear contact lenses

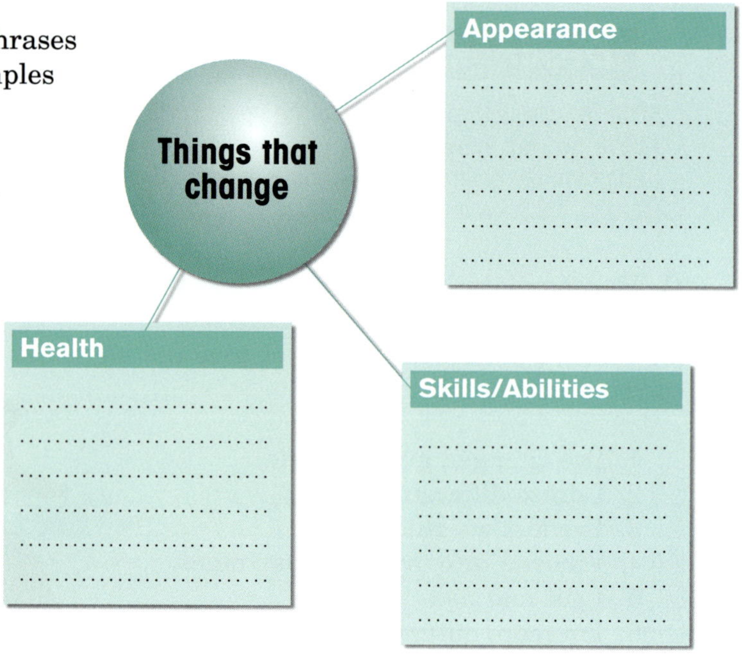

B ***Pair work*** Have you changed in any of these areas? Tell your partner about a change in each category.

"I get up earlier in the morning. I've started cooking. And I get dressed up for work now."

6 CONVERSATION *Planning your future*

A Listen and practice.

Alex: So what are you going to do after graduation, Susan?
Susan: Well, I've saved some money, and I think I'd really like to travel.
Alex: Lucky you. That sounds exciting!
Susan: Yeah. Then I plan to get a job and my own apartment.
Alex: Oh, you're not going to live at home?
Susan: No, I don't want to live with my parents – not after I start to work.
Alex: I know what you mean.
Susan: What about you, Alex? Do you have any plans yet?
Alex: I'm going to get a job *and* live at home. I'm broke, and I want to pay off my student loan!

CLASS AUDIO ONLY

B Listen to the rest of the conversation.

1. What kind of job does Alex want?
2. Where would Susan like to travel?

7 GRAMMAR FOCUS

Verb + infinitive

What **are** you **going to do** after graduation?
I'm (not) **going to get** a job right away.
I (don't) **plan to get** my own apartment.
I (don't) **want to live** with my parents.
I **hope to get** a new car.
I'd like to travel this summer.
I'd love to move to a new city.

A Complete these statements so that they are true for you. Use information from the grammar box. Then add three more statements of your own.

1. I .... move to a new city.
2. I .... get married.
3. I .... have a large family.
4. I .... find a job where I can travel.
5. I .... make a lot of money!
6. I .... become very successful.
7. I .... retire at an early age.
8. ....
9. ....
10. ....

B ***Pair work*** Compare your responses with a partner. How are you the same? How are you different?

8 PLAN ON IT

Group work What are your plans for the future? Ask and answer these questions.

What are you going to do after this English course is over?
Do you plan to study here again next year?
What other languages would you like to learn?
What countries would you like to live in? Why?
What countries wouldn't you like to live in? Why?
Do you want to get a (new) job in a few years?
What kind of job do you hope to get?

9 PRONUNCIATION *Reduced form of* to

A Listen and practice. Notice that **to** is reduced to /tə/.

I hope **to** get married.
I plan **to** have a large family.
I'd love **to** move to a new city.
I'd like **to** live in a small town.

B ***Pair work*** Write four statements about yourself using the verbs above. Take turns reading your statements with a partner. Pay attention to the pronunciation of **to**.

10 WRITING

A Write about your plans for the future.

I would like to join the Peace Corps for a couple of years. I have a degree in biology, so I hope to work in forestry or environmental education. I'd like to work with people in . . . .

working in the Peace Corps

B ***Pair work*** Compare your composition with a partner's. Ask and answer questions about each other's plans.

interchange 16

Unfold your future!

Imagine you could do anything, go anywhere, and meet anybody.
Turn to page IC-21.

11 LISTENING

CLASS AUDIO ONLY

A Listen to three people discussing their plans for the future. What do they plan to do? What don't they want to do? Take notes.

	Plans to	Doesn't want to
1. Charlie		
2. Loon		
3. Marie		

B ***Group work*** Which person do you think is most like you? Do your classmates agree?

12 READING

The Future Looks Bright

Do you like to set goals for yourself? What important goals have you reached recently?

Balamurati Krishna Ambati

At age three, Balamurati Krishna Ambati was badly burned and spent several months in the hospital. He decided then that he wanted to be a doctor. A few years later, he read in the *Guinness Book of Records* that the youngest doctor in the world was 18 years old. So he decided to become a doctor by the age of 17. Many people thought this was impossible, but at 11, Ambati was in college. He graduated from college at 14 and from medical school at 17. Now that he is a doctor, Ambati plans to go for advanced training in Boston.

Catherine Charlton

Catherine Charlton is studying engineering at Cornell University, but she has already achieved an important goal: She has worked for NASA (the National Aeronautics and Space Administration). Charlton's achievements aren't only in engineering, however. She is also a successful pianist and composer. Charlton hopes to combine her talents for engineering and music someday. For example, she would like to design concert halls or manufacture pianos.

Jasmin Sethi

The Scholastic Aptitude Test is the test American students take to enter college; each year, only a few students get a perfect score. One of those students was Jasmin Sethi. Her achievement was especially remarkable because she is blind. To take the test, someone read the test questions to her, and she gave the answers. She even solved difficult math problems in her head. Sethi has been the editor of her school newspaper and has organized food collections. She wants to go to a top university next year. Sethi would like to be a lawyer.

A Read the article. What are each student's interests? What goals has each student set?

	Interests	Goals
1. Balamurati	....	....
2. Catherine	....	....
3. Jasmin	....	....

B ***Pair work*** Talk about these questions.

1. Do you think Balamurati is too young to be a doctor?
2. What other careers would allow Catherine to combine her interests?
3. How do you think someone like Jasmin overcomes his or her disabilities?
4. How old were you when you started to think about your career goals?
5. Have you achieved a goal you set? What was it?
6. What other goals do you have?

Review of Units 13–16

1 FAVORITE RESTAURANT

A *Group work* Take turns talking about your favorite place to eat. One student makes a statement about a favorite restaurant. Other students ask questions.

My favorite place to eat is . . . .

Where is it?
What kind of food do they serve?
Does it have a nice atmosphere?
Is it expensive?
How much does dinner cost?
When is it open?
How often do you go there?
What do you usually order?

B *Class activity* Which place is the most interesting to you? Tell the class why.

2 LISTENING

CLASS AUDIO ONLY

Listen and check (✓) the best response.

1. ☐ Yes, this way, please.
   ☐ Yes, please.
2. ☐ No, I don't.
   ☐ Yes, I'll have tea, please.
3. ☐ I'd like a steak, please.
   ☐ Yes, I would.
4. ☐ I'll have a cup of coffee.
   ☐ Italian, please.
5. ☐ Carrots, please.
   ☐ Yes, I will.
6. ☐ Yes, I'd like some water.
   ☐ No, I don't think so.

3 INTERESTING ADDRESSES

A *Pair work* Ask and answer questions about these places in your city.

Buildings	*Streets*	*Entertainment*
the biggest hotel	the busiest street	the best place to go dancing
the most famous building	the best street for restaurants	the best place to listen to music
the oldest building	the best street for shopping	the most interesting tourist spot

A: What's the biggest hotel?
B: I think it's the Hilton.
A: I do, too. / So do I. /
Oh, I don't. I think it's the . . . .

B *Class activity* Compare your answers around the class.

4 THE WEEKEND

Pair work Which of the activities listed are you going to do this weekend? What else are you going to do? Talk with a partner.

A: I'm seeing a concert this weekend.
B: What concert are you going to see?
A: A guitar concert at school.
B: Really? When is it?
A: It's on Saturday night. I'm going with my brother.

Some activities

see a concert
meet someone special
go out to eat
work
play a sport or exercise
make a long-distance call

5 ROLE PLAY *Inviting a friend*

A ***Pair work*** Take turns inviting your partner to do something.

A: Hello?
B: Hi, ... This is . . . .
A: Oh, hi!
B: Say, are you doing anything (on) . . . ?
A: Oh, yes. I'm sorry. I'm . . . .
B: Well, how about (on) . . . ?
A: No. What would you like to do?
B: Let's . . . .
A: I'd love to! What time . . . ?
B: . . .
A: And where . . . ?
B: . . .
A: OK. See you on . . . . Bye!
B: Bye-bye.

B ***Pair work*** Change roles and try the conversation with a different partner.

6 INTERVIEW

A ***Pair work*** Find out more about a classmate. Ask your partner these questions or questions of your own.

Where have you lived?
What schools have you gone to?
What did you study? / What do you study now?
Are you married? / Do you hope to get married?
Do you have any children? / Do you want to have children?
What would you like to do in five years? ten years? when you retire?

B ***Class activity*** Tell the class about your partner.

Interchange Activities

interchange 1 GETTING TO KNOW YOU

A ***Class activity*** Go around the class and find this information. Write a classmate's name only once.

Find someone who . . .	Name
1. . . . has the same first name as a famous person. **"What's your first name?"**	....
2. . . . has an unusual nickname. **"What do people call you?"**	....
3. . . . has an interesting middle name. **"What's your middle name?"**	....
4. . . . has the same last name as a famous person. **"What's your last name?"**	....
5. . . . is named after his or her father or mother. **"Are you named after your father or mother?"**	....
6. . . . always remembers people's names. **"Are you good with names?"**	....
7. . . . is from a beautiful city or town. **"Where are you from?"**	....
8. . . . speaks two foreign languages. **"What languages do you speak?"**	....

B ***Pair work*** Compare your information with a partner.

interchange 2 COMMON GROUND

A Complete this chart with information about yourself.

	Time
I usually get up at	....
I have breakfast at	....
I leave for work or school at	....
I have dinner at	....
I go to bed during the week at	....
I go to bed on weekends at	....

B ***Class activity*** Take a survey. Ask five classmates for this information.

Names:	....	....	....	....	....
What time do you . . . ?	**Times**				
get up	....	....	....	....	....
have breakfast	....	....	....	....	....
leave for work or school	....	....	....	....	....
have dinner	....	....	....	....	....
go to bed during the week	....	....	....	....	....
go to bed on weekends	....	....	....	....	....

C ***Class activity*** Compare the times you do things with the times your classmates do things. Whose schedule is the most like yours? Tell the class.

"Keiko and I have a similar schedule. We both get up at six and have breakfast at seven A.M. . . ."

useful expressions

We both . . . at . . . .
We . . . at different times.
My schedule isn't like anyone else's.

interchange 3 *SWAP MEET*

Student A

A You want to sell these things. Write an appropriate price for each item.

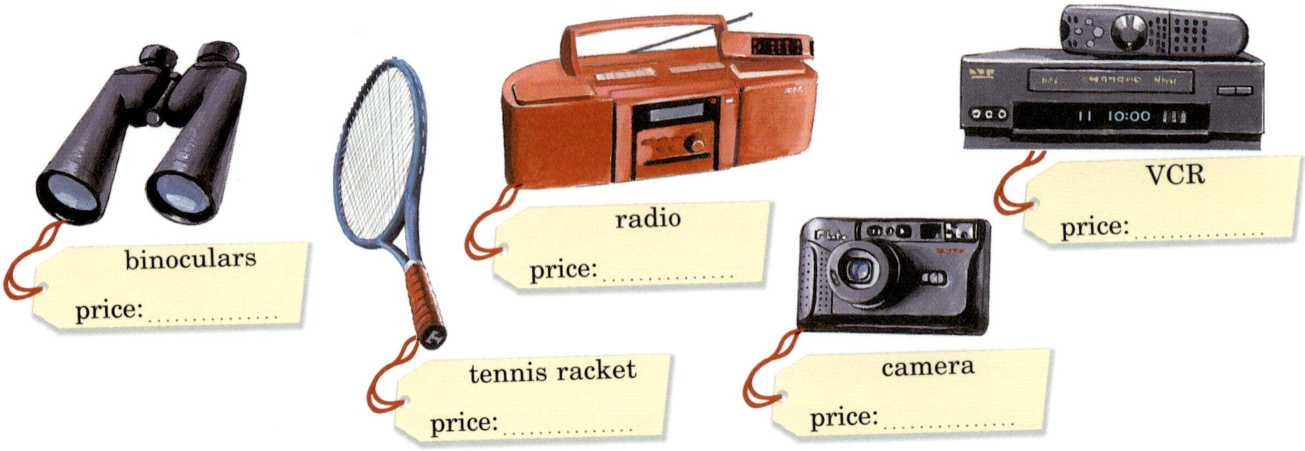

Student B

A You want to sell these things. Write an appropriate price for each item.

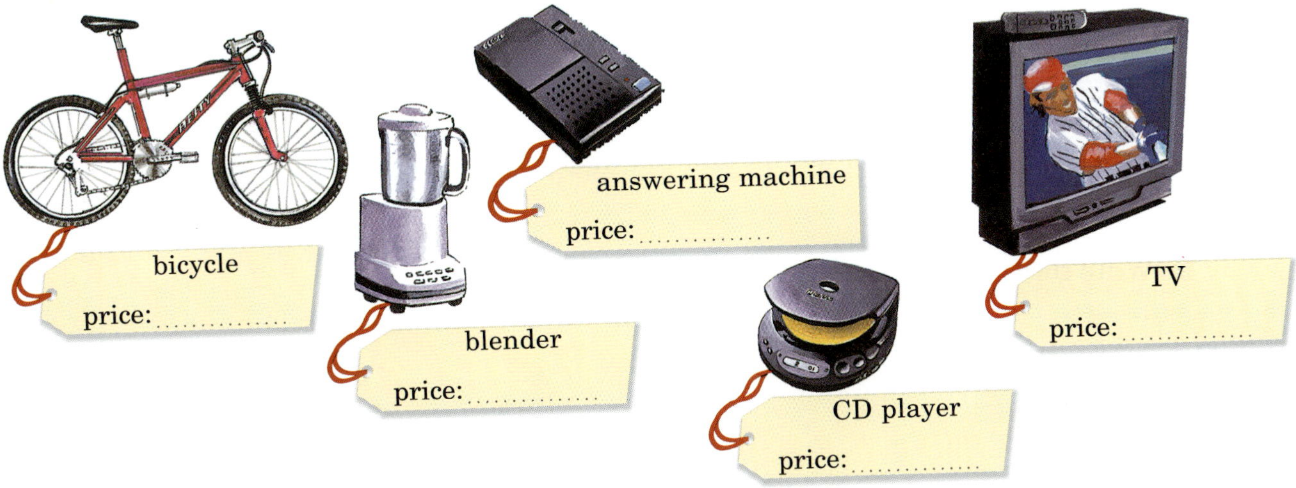

Students A and B

B ***Pair work*** Discuss the price of each thing and choose at least three things that you want to buy. Get the best price you can. Be prepared to haggle.*

A: How much is the . . . ?
B: It's only $ . . . .
A: Wow! That's expensive!
B: Well, how about $ . . . ?
A: No. That's still too much. What about the . . . ?
B: You can have it for $ . . . .
A: OK. That's reasonable.
B: And how much is the . . . ?
A: . . .

* *haggle:* Buyers and sellers suggest other amounts until both agree on a lower price.

interchange 4 *WHAT AN INVITATION! WHAT AN EXCUSE!*

A Make up three invitations to interesting or unusual activities. Write them on cards.

<u>Godzilla Meets Mightyman</u> is at the Plaza Theater tonight at 8:00. Would you like to see it?	*There's a dog and cat show at City Stadium on Saturday. It's at 3:00. Do you want to go?*	*I want to see the Turtle Races tomorrow. They're at 1:00 at the Civic Hall. Would you like to go?*

B Write three response cards. One is an acceptance card.

That sounds great! What time do you want to meet?

The other two cards are refusals. Think of silly or unusual excuses.

I'd like to, but I want to take my bird to a singing contest.	*I'm sorry. I'd like to, but I have to wash my hair.*

C ***Class activity*** Put all the invitation cards in one pile and all the response cards in another pile facedown. Shuffle each pile. Each student takes three invitation cards and three response cards.

Go around the class. Invite people to do the things on your invitation cards. Use the response cards to accept or decline any invitation.

interchange 5 FAMILY FACTS

A ***Class activity*** Go around the class and find this information.
Write a classmate's name only once. Ask follow-up questions of your own.

Find someone . . .	Name
1. . . . who is an only child. **"Do you have any brothers or sisters?"**	....
2. . . . who has more than two brothers. **"How many brothers do you have?"**	....
3. . . . who has more than two sisters. **"How many sisters do you have?"**	....
4. . . . whose brother or sister is studying abroad. **"Are any of your brothers or sisters studying abroad? Where?"**	....
5. . . . who lives with his or her grandparents. **"Do you live with your grandparents?"**	....
6. . . . who has a great-grandparent still living. **"Is your great-grandmother or great-grandfather still living?"**	....
7. . . . who has a family member with an unusual job. **"Does anyone in your family have an unusual job?"**	....
8. . . . whose mother or father is working abroad. **"Is either of your parents working abroad? Where?"**	....

B ***Group work*** Compare your information in groups.

interchange 6 FITNESS QUIZ

A ***Pair work*** Interview a partner using this simple quiz. Then add up your partner's score, and find his or her rank below.

Fitness Quiz

Your Nutrition

	Points
1. How many meals do you eat during a day?	
• Five or six small meals	6
• Three meals	3
• One or two meals	0
2. Do you eat at regular times during the day (not too early or too late)?	
• Almost always	6
• Usually	3
• Seldom	0
3. How many servings of fruits and vegetables do you usually have a day?	
• Five or more	6
• Two to four	4
• One or none	1
4. How much fatty food do you eat?	
• Very little	6
• About average	3
• A lot	0
5. Do you take vitamins every day?	
• Always	6
• Often	4
• Sometimes	2
6. Do you take more vitamins when you are sick?	
• Yes	4
• No	2

Rank your partner.

55 to 70 points: Super job! Keep up the good work!

35 to 54 points: Good job! Your health and fitness are above average.

15 to 34 points: Your health and fitness are below average. Try to learn more about health and fitness.

14 points and below: You seem to be out of shape. Now is the time to start making changes. See your doctor or other professionals if you need help.

Your Fitness

	Points
7. How often do you exercise?	
• Three or more days a week	6
• One or two days a week	3
• Never	0
8. Which best describes your fitness program?	
• Both weight training and aerobic exercise	6
• Weight training or aerobic exercise only	3
• None	0
9. How important is your fitness program to you?	
• Very important	6
• Somewhat important	3
• Not very important	0

Your Health

	Points
10. Which best describes your weight?	
• Within 6 pounds (3 kg) of my ideal weight	6
• Within 10 pounds (4.5 kg) of my ideal weight	3
• More than 12 pounds (5.5 kg) over or under	0
11. How often do you have a complete physical?	
• Once a year	6
• Every two or three years	3
• Almost never go to the doctor	0
12. How often do you smoke?	
• Never	6
• Hardly ever	1
• Often	0

Total Points ______

B ***Group work*** Compare your scores in groups. Who is the fittest? What can you do to improve your fitness?

"I need to . . . ."

interchange 7 VACATION PHOTOS

Student A

A ***Pair work*** You went on a vacation to Mexico and took these photos. First, think about these questions. Then use the photos to tell your partner about your vacation. Give as much information as you can, and answer your partner's questions.

"I had a really interesting vacation. I went to Mexico . . . ."

Where did you go?
How long were you there?
Who did you go with?
What did you do there?
Did you enjoy it?
Where did you take this picture?
Who is this/that?
Is this a . . . ?

Mexico City – a beautiful night
shopping
a bullfighter
the Pyramid of the Moon
some Mariachis

B ***Pair work*** Listen to your partner talk about his or her vacation. Ask questions like the ones in part A about the vacation.

interchange 7 *VACATION PHOTOS*

Student B

A ***Pair work*** Listen to your partner talk about a recent vacation. Ask questions about the vacation and the photos.

Where did you go?
How long were you there?
Who did you go with?
What did you do there?
Did you enjoy it?
Where did you take this picture?
Who is this/that?
Is this a . . . ?

B ***Pair work*** Look at these photos of your vacation in Thailand. First, think about the questions in part A. Then use the photos to tell your partner about your vacation. Give as much information as you can, and answer your partner's questions.

"I had a really interesting vacation recently, too. I went to Thailand . . . ."

interchange 8 NEIGHBORHOOD SURVEY

A ***Group work*** Imagine you are looking for a new home. You need to decide where you want to live. Compare two different neighborhoods in your city or town. Talk with your group and complete the survey.

What kinds of people live in each neighborhood – families, young people, working people, retired people?
Compare the neighborhoods' recreation facilities, stores, schools, and public transportation.
How much noise is there? pollution?
What's one advantage of living in each neighborhood? What's one disadvantage?

	Neighborhood 1:	Neighborhood 2:
	....	....
people		
recreation facilities		
stores		
schools		
public transportation		
noise		
pollution		
an advantage of living in the neighborhood		
a disadvantage of living in the neighborhood		

A: What neighborhoods do you want to compare?
B: Let's look at Parkside and downtown.
C: OK. So what kinds of people live in Parkside?
D: There are lots of retired people. There aren't very many young people with families.
A: That's true. What about downtown?
C: . . .

B ***Class activity*** Study the results of the survey. Which neighborhood would you prefer to live in? Tell the class where and why.

interchange 9 FIND THE DIFFERENCES

Student A

A ***Pair work*** How many differences can you find between your picture here and your partner's picture? Ask questions like these to find the differences. (Look only at the people with names.)

How many people are there in your picture?
How many are standing? Who?
How many are sitting? Who?
What color is Dave's T-shirt? Kate's sweater?
Who is holding a drink?
What does . . . look like?
Does . . . wear glasses?
Does . . . have a beard?
What color is . . .'s hair?
How long is . . .'s hair?

Picture 1

B ***Class activity*** How many differences are there in the pictures? What are they?

"In picture 1, Dave's T-shirt is . . . . In picture 2, it's . . . ."

interchange 10 LIFESTYLES SURVEY

A ***Pair work*** What kind of lifestyle does your partner have: easygoing and relaxed or busy and fast-paced? Interview your partner using this survey.

Easygoing and relaxed?

How many times have you . . .	Number of times
1. watched TV in the past week?	....
2. slept late in the past two weeks?	....
3. read a book in the last month?	....
4. been to a movie in the last two months?	....
5. written a letter to a friend in the last six months?	....

Busy and fast-paced?

How many times have you . . .	Number of times
6. eaten a takeout meal in the past week?	....
7. gotten home late in the evening in the last two weeks?	....
8. played sports or exercised in the last month?	....
9. worked late or studied past midnight in the last month?	....
10. been to a party in the last six months?	....

B ***Group work*** Tell the group what you think your partner's lifestyle is like and why.

"Juan's lifestyle is busy and fast-paced. He hardly ever has time to watch TV, read a book, or go to the movies. He works late a lot, and he often eats takeout meals. . . . "

interchange 9 FIND THE DIFFERENCES

Student B

A ***Pair work*** How many differences can you find between your picture here and your partner's picture? Ask questions like these to find the differences. (Look only at the people with names.)

How many people are there in your picture?
How many are standing? Who?
How many are sitting? Who?
What color is Dave's T-shirt? Kate's sweater?
Who is holding a drink?
What does . . . look like?
Does . . . wear glasses?
Does . . . have a beard?
What color is . . .'s hair?
How long is . . .'s hair?

Picture 2

B ***Class activity*** How many differences are there in the pictures? What are they?

"In picture 1, Dave's T-shirt is . . . . In picture 2, it's . . . ."

interchange 11 *CITY GUIDE*

A Where can you get information about your city? buy souvenirs? see historical sights? Complete the "City Guide" with information about your city.

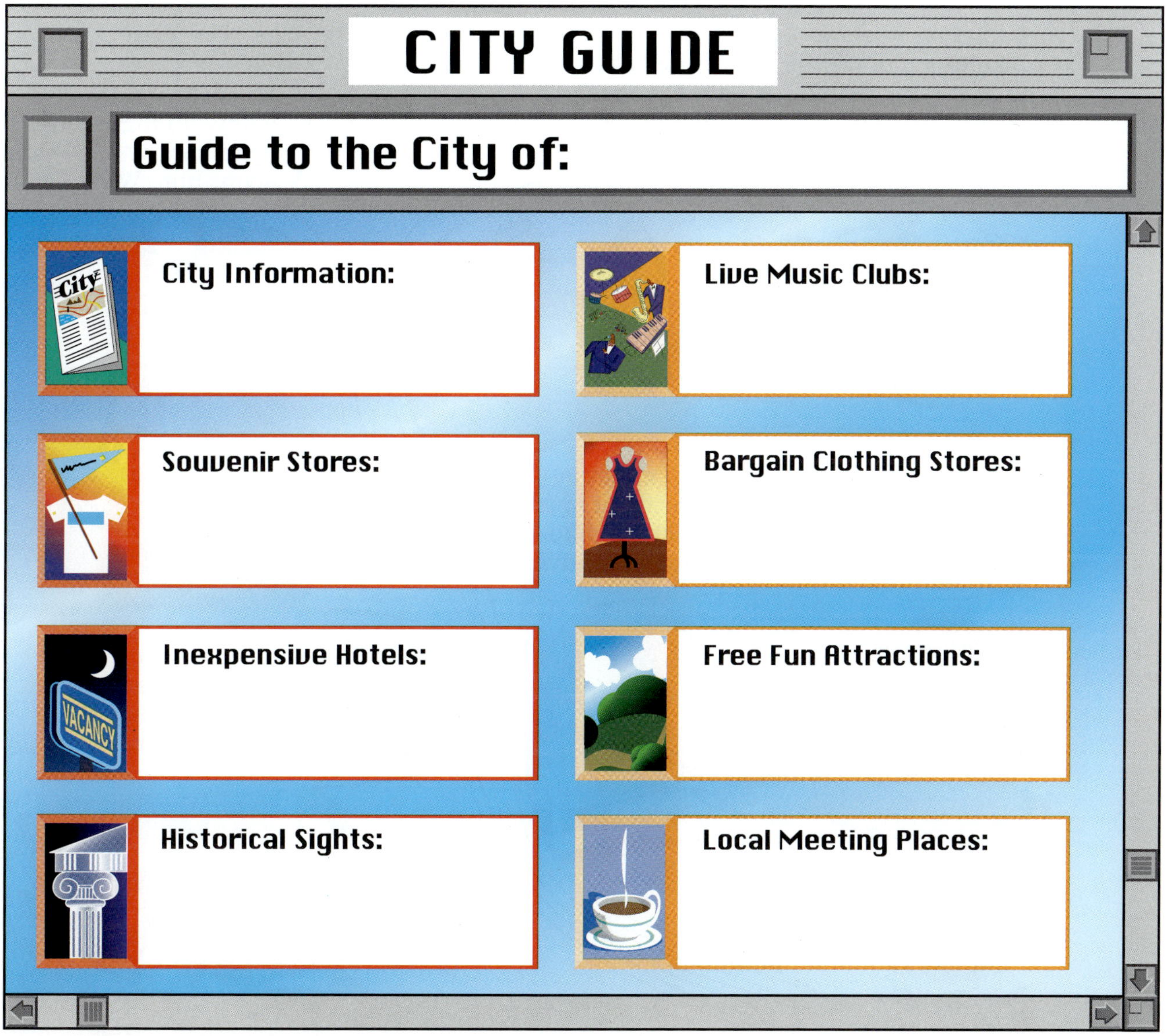

B ***Group work*** Compare your "City Guides" in groups. Ask these questions and your own questions. Add any additional or interesting information to your guide.

Where can you get information about your city?
Where can you buy souvenirs?
Are there any inexpensive hotels?
What historical sights should you see?
What's a good place to hear local music?
What's a cheap place to shop for clothes?
What fun things can you do for free?
Where do people often meet?

interchange 12 TALK RADIO

A ***Group work*** Look at the four questions that people called a radio program about. What advice would you give each caller? Discuss suggestions to give each caller, and then choose the best one.

useful expressions

I think it would be useful to . . . .
One thing you could do is . . . .
It's a good idea to . . . .
It's important to . . . .
You should . . . .

B ***Class activity*** Share your group's advice for each problem with the class.

interchange 13 ARE YOU READY TO ORDER?

Student A

You are the waiter or waitress at The Corner Cafe. Take your customers' orders.

Taking the order

- Greet your customers.
- Ask what they would like. Write down each person's order on a separate piece of paper. (Use the menu to write down the orders and amounts.)
- Check the orders like this: "You ordered . . . ." and "You wanted . . . ."
- Ask if your customers want anything else (such as something to drink, a salad, or dessert).
- Go and get their orders.

Delivering the order

- Bring the orders to your customers. (You make a mistake. You give one customer the wrong thing.)
- Go and get the right order and bring it back.

Bringing the check

- Give each customer his or her check with a total at the bottom. (You make a mistake. You did not correctly add up one of the checks.)
- Walk away and wait for the customers to put the checks and money on the table.
- Pick up the checks and money. Bring back each customer's change.

The Corner Cafe

Soups	Cup/Bowl
Chicken Noodle	$2.00/$3.00
Clam Chowder	$2.00/$3.00
French Onion	$3.00/$4.50

Sandwiches (served with Cole Slaw)	
Tuna Salad	$4.25
Roast Beef	$4.75
Grilled Chicken Breast	$6.95

Beverages	Medium/Large
Coffee or Tea	$.50/$1.00
Soda	$.75/$1.25
Iced Tea	$1.00/$1.50
Milk	$.75/$1.25

Salads	
Mixed Greens	$1.50
Pasta Salad	$2.75
Chef Salad	$4.25

Burgers (served with French Fries)	
Hamburger	$5.50
Cheeseburger	$6.00
Turkey Burger	$5.75

Desserts	
Ice Cream (Chocolate, Vanilla, or Strawberry)	$1.50
Apple Pie	$2.25
Chocolate Cake	$3.75

interchange 13 ARE YOU READY TO ORDER?

Students B and C

You are hungry customers in The Corner Cafe. You are having lunch. The waiter or waitress comes to take your order.

Ordering
- Look at the menu below. Order something to eat and drink.
- Ask the waiter or waitress to bring you something extra (such as a glass of water or another fork).

Being served
- The waiter or waitress brings your order. Is it correct? If not, tell him or her like this: "Sorry, I didn't order . . . . I ordered . . . ."

Paying the check
- The waiter or waitress brings a check for each of you. Are they correct? If not, tell him or her like this: "Excuse me. This isn't right. It should be . . . ."
- Put the checks and money on the table for the waiter or waitress to pick up.

Tipping
- The waiter or waitress brings your change.
- Decide how much to leave for a tip.

The Corner Cafe

Soups	*Cup / Bowl*
Chicken Noodle	$2.00/$3.00
Clam Chowder	$2.00/$3.00
French Onion	$3.00/$4.50

Sandwiches *(served with Cole Slaw)*	
Tuna Salad	$4.25
Roast Beef	$4.75
Grilled Chicken Breast	$6.95

Beverages	*Medium / Large*
Coffee or Tea	$.50/$1.00
Soda	$.75/$1.25
Iced Tea	$1.00/$1.50
Milk	$.75/$1.25

Salads	
Mixed Greens	$1.50
Pasta Salad	$2.75
Chef Salad	$4.25

Burgers *(served with French Fries)*	
Hamburger	$5.50
Cheeseburger	$6.00
Turkey Burger	$5.75

Desserts	
Ice Cream (Chocolate, Vanilla, or Strawberry)	$1.50
Apple Pie	$2.25
Chocolate Cake	$3.75

interchange 14 HOW MUCH DO YOU KNOW?

Pair work Take turns asking and answering these questions. Check (✓) the correct answer. If you and your partner don't agree, check (✓) the answer you think is correct.

World Knowledge Quiz

1.	Which metal is the heaviest?	☐ gold	☐ silver	☐ aluminum
2.	Which planet is the coldest?	☐ Neptune	☐ Saturn	☐ Pluto
3.	Which one is the biggest?	☐ Jupiter	☐ the Earth	☐ Mars
4.	Which animal lives the longest?	☐ a whale	☐ an elephant	☐ a tortoise
5.	Which one is the tallest?	☐ an elephant	☐ a giraffe	☐ a camel
6.	Which of these is the heaviest?	☐ the brain	☐ the heart	☐ the liver
7.	Which drink has the most calories?	☐ 1 liter of wine	☐ 1 liter of beer	☐ 1 liter of soda*
8.	Which country is the driest?	☐ Egypt	☐ Peru	☐ Chile
9.	Which one is closest to the equator?	☐ Malaysia	☐ Colombia	☐ India
10.	Which shape has the most sides?	☐ a pentagon	☐ an octagon	☐ a hexagon
11.	Which measurement is the longest?	☐ a yard	☐ a kilometer	☐ a mile
12.	Which era is the oldest?	☐ the Renaissance	☐ the Dark Ages	☐ the Middle Ages

*1 liter = 35 ounces

Correct answers

How many did you get correct? (See the appendix at the back of the book for the answers.)

12 Perfect! Brilliant! You should be a teacher.
9–11 Very good! Do you watch lots of TV game shows?
5–8 Just OK. How often do you go to the library?
0–4 You should never be on a quiz show.

interchange 15 *WHAT ARE YOU GOING TO DO?*

A ***Class activity*** What are your classmates' plans for the weekend? Go around the class and find people who are going to do these things. Ask for further information.

Find someone who is going to . . . next weekend.	Name
go on a date	....
stay out all night	....
go to an amusement park	....
go to a party	....
visit friends out of town	....
compete in a sports event	....
see a play	....
go to a garage sale	....

A: Are you going to an amusement park this weekend?

OR

A: Are you going to go to an amusement park this weekend?
B: Yes, I am, actually.
A: Oh, you are? Who are you going with?
B: . . .

B ***Pair work*** Compare your information with a partner.

interchange 16 UNFOLD YOUR FUTURE!

A Complete this chart with information about yourself.

My Possible Future	
What are two things you plan to do next year?	....
	....
What are two things you aren't going to do next year?	....
	....
What is something you would like to change?	....
	....
What is something you hope to buy in the next year?	....
	....
What is a place you want to visit someday?	....
What is a place you would like to move to?	....
Who would you like to take a vacation with?	....
What famous person would you like to meet?	....

B ***Group work*** Compare your information in groups. Be prepared to explain the future you have planned.

A: What are two things you plan to do next year?
B: Well, I'm going to travel to Italy and meet someone new.
C: Oh, really? Who are you going to meet?
B: I don't know, yet! What about you? What are two things you plan to do next year?
C: . . .

Unit Summaries

Unit Summaries contain lists of key vocabulary and functional expressions, as well as grammar extensions for each unit. For Grammar Focus models, please refer to the appropriate unit page.

1 PLEASE CALL ME CHUCK.

KEY VOCABULARY

Nouns
back
bow
cheek
class
Dad
engineering
female
friend
greeting
handshake
hug
kiss
male
Mom
(first/last/full) name
nickname
parents
pat
student
(baseball/volleyball) team
women

Titles
Miss
Mr.
Mrs.
Ms.

Adjectives
married
same
single

Articles
a
the

Verbs
am
are
is

Adverbs
here
(over) there
too

Prepositions
from (Paris/France)
in (English 102/Canada)
on (the volleyball team/
the back)

Conjunctions
and
but

Interjections
oh
well

EXPRESSIONS

Greeting someone
Hello.
Hi.

Exchanging personal information
What's your name?
I'm . . . . /My name is . . . .
Where are you from?
I'm from . . . .
How's everything?/
How are you?
Not bad.
Pretty good, thanks.

Introducing someone
This is . . . . /These are . . . .
Nice to/Pleased to/
Good to meet you.

Asking about someone
Who's that?
That's . . . .
Who are they?
Their names are . . . and . . . .

Checking information
How do you pronounce . . . ?
It's Mandel, with the accent on "del."
How do you spell . . . ?
What do people call you?
Please call me . . . .
You can call me . . . .
Everyone calls me . . . .
Excuse me, what's . . . again?
It's . . . .
Are you studying . . . ?/
Are you on vacation?
Yes, I am./No, I'm not.

Agreeing
That's right.
OK.

GRAMMAR EXTENSION Sentences with be

My name **is** Amy.
be + noun

I **am** from Korea.
be + prepositional phrase

I **am** Korean.
be + adjective

2 HOW DO YOU SPEND YOUR DAY?

KEY VOCABULARY

Nouns
Jobs/Professions
announcer
architect
carpenter
chef
company director
disc jockey
doctor
engineer
flight attendant
(tour) guide
nurse
police officer
professor
receptionist
sales manager
salesman
salesperson
secretary
security guard
supervisor
teacher
travel agent
word processor

Workplaces
airline
(construction/
electronics)
company
department store
hospital
office
radio station
(fast-food)
restaurant
school

Classes
business
computer science
mathematics

Time
day
holiday
hour
week
year

Other
clothes
country
(computer)
equipment
food
high school
house
instruction
lunch
music
(news)paper
passenger
patient
people
phone
snack
tour
TV
weather report
work

Adjectives
average
full-time
great
interesting
little
long
part-time

Article
an

Verbs
answer
arrive (at)
build
care for
cook
do
get (home)
get up
go (to bed/to
school/to work)
have (a job/lunch)
leave
like
love
play (music)
read
sell
serve
sleep
sound (interesting)
spend (your day)
start
stay up
study
take
teach
wake up
watch
work

Adverbs
a lot
early
exactly
home
late
only
pretty (late)
then

Prepositions
about/around
(10:00/noon)
after (midnight)
at (night/7:00/
noon/midnight)
before (noon)
for (an hour)
in (the morning/
the afternoon/
the evening)
like (Peru)
on (weekends/
weekdays/
weeknights/
Sundays)
until (midnight)

Interjection
so

EXPRESSIONS

Describing work/school
What do you do?
I'm a/an . . . .
Where do you work?
I work at/in/for . . . .
Where do you go to school?
I go to . . . .

Asking for more information
What about . . . ?
Which . . . ?

Asking for and giving opinions
How do you like . . . ?
I like . . . a lot./I love . . . .
It's a great . . . .

Expressing interest
Really?
Oh, really?
That sounds interesting.

Talking about daily schedules
How do you spend your day?
Well, I . . . . Then I . . . .
What time do you go to work/school?
I leave at . . . .
And when do you get home?
I get home around . . . .

Apologizing
Gee, I'm sorry.

GRAMMAR EXTENSION

1. Prepositions in sentences about work/school

I work **for** Toyota.	*for* + name of company
for Ms. Jones.	*for* + name of person
for a lawyer.	*for* + person's job
I work **in** a bank.	*in/at* + workplace
at a restaurant.	
I work **in** the sales department.	*in* + department/section
in the front office.	
I go **to** Columbia University.	*to* + name of school

2. Articles

Indefinite articles

I'm **a** student.	*a* before consonants
He's **an** engineer.	*an* before vowel sounds

Definite article

I work for **the** *Daily News*.	*the* + specific place
in **the** sales department.	

3 HOW MUCH IS IT?

KEY VOCABULARY

Nouns
Clothes and jewelry
backpack
bag
boots
bracelet
cap
earrings
gloves
jacket
(pair of) jeans
necklace
pants
ring
Rollerblades
scarf
shirt
(athletic) shoes
sunglasses
sweater
tie
watch

*Materials**
cotton
gold
leather
plastic
polyester
rubber
silk
silver
wool

*Names of materials can be used as nouns or adjectives.

Other
adult
color
compact disc
cost
(room) decor
design
dollar
entertainment
(for) example
expenses
(gallon of) gas
haircut
health
money
(birthday) present
price
salary
savings
style
(price) tag
taxes
thing
transportation

Adjectives
attractive
bad
big
cheap
dark
different
each
expensive
good
large
light
medium
nice
OK
perfect
pretty
reasonable
small
warm
yearly

Verbs
buy
get
have on
let (me) + verb
look (= seem)
look at
pay (for)
prefer
spend (money)
try on

Adverbs
almost
better
more
right there

Preposition
for (you)

Conjunction
or

EXPRESSIONS

Talking about prices
How much is this sweater ?
  It's . . . .
That isn't bad.
How much are those shoes?
  They're . . . .
That's expensive.

Comparing
The black boots are more attractive/prettier than the brown ones.

Identifying things
Which one?
  The wool one.
Which ones?
  The blue ones.

Talking about preferences
Which one do you like better/more?
  I like the . . . one better/more.
Which ones do you prefer?
  I prefer the . . . ones.

Getting someone's attention
Excuse me.
Hey.
Look!

Making and declining an offer
Would you like to . . . ?
  Oh, no. That's OK.

Thanking someone
Thank you (anyway).
  You're welcome.

Asking for more information
Why?
Do you mean . . . ?
Oh, these?

Expressing doubt
Hmm.
I'm not sure.

Expressing surprise
Are you kidding?

GRAMMAR EXTENSION Comparative of adjectives

Adjectives with -er

Add *-er:*	cheap → cheap**er**
Add *-r:*	nice → nice**r**
Drop *y* and add *-ier:*	pretty → prett**ier**
Double the final consonant and add *-er:*	big → big**ger**

Adjectives with more
more + adjective: **more** perfect
more expensive

For more information on comparatives, see the appendix at the back of the book.

4 DO YOU LIKE JAZZ?

KEY VOCABULARY

Nouns
*Music**
classical
country
gospel
jazz
New Age
pop
rap/urban
rock
salsa

*Names of musical styles can be used as nouns or adjectives.

Movies
comedy
horror film
science fiction
thriller
western

TV programs
game show
news
soap opera
talk show

Entertainers
actor
actress
group
singer

Other
CD
date
dinner
fan
(baseball) game
gym
kind (of)
piano
play
theater
ticket
trumpet
video

Adjectives
best
favorite
new

Verbs
agree
ask
come over
go out
have to
know
listen to
meet
need
play (an instrument)
save
sing
think of
visit
want

Adverbs
just
really
tonight

Prepositions
for (dinner)
on (TV)
with (me)

EXPRESSIONS

Talking about likes and dislikes
Do you like . . . ?
 Yes, I do. I like . . . a lot.
 No, I don't. I can't stand . . . .
 No, I don't like . . . very much.
What kind of . . . do you like?
What do you think of . . . ?
What's/Who's your favorite . . . ?

Giving opinions
I like . . . . Do you?
I can't stand . . . . How about you?
I think . . . .
We don't agree on . . . .

Inviting and accepting/ refusing invitations
Would you like to . . . ?
 Yes, I would./I'd love to.
Do you want to . . . ?
 That sounds great.
 I'd like to, but I have to . . . .

Making suggestions
Why don't you . . . ?
Let's . . . .
 That sounds fine.

Asking about events
When is it?
Where is it?
What time does it start?
Where should we . . . ?

Asking for more information
How about . . . ?

GRAMMAR EXTENSION

1. Plural nouns

Add *-s:*	singer →	singer**s**
Add *-es:*	actress →	actress**es**
Drop *y* and add *-ies:*	comedy →	comed**ies**

2. Prepositions

Do you want to go out **on** Saturday?	*on* + day
Let's meet **at** the theater.	*at* + place
at 7:30.	*at* + time

5 TELL ME ABOUT YOUR FAMILY.

KEY VOCABULARY

Nouns
Family/Relatives
aunt
brother
children
cousin
daughter
father
grandfather
grandmother
grandparents
husband
mother
nephew
niece
sister
sister-in-law
son
uncle
wife

Other
acting
age
college
exhibition
fact
family tree
headline
home
(foreign) language
lawyer
painter
percent
semester
theater company
winter

Pronoun
anyone

Adjectives
divorced
elderly
famous
together
young

Verbs
break up
end
get (married/divorced)
live
look for
move
remarry
return
say
stay
take (a class)
take care of
talk
tell
travel
visit

Adverbs
Time expressions
again
ever
most of the time
never
(right) now
often
still
these days
usually
this month/semester/
winter/year

Other
abroad
alone

Prepositions
at (a university/home)
by (the age of . . .)

EXPRESSIONS

Asking about someone
Tell me about . . . .
What is . . . doing these days?

Exchanging information about the present
Are you still looking for a job?
Yes, I am./No, I'm not.
What are you studying this year?
I'm studying a foreign language.
Is anyone in your family . . . right now?
Yes, my . . . is.

Expressing interest
Is that right?
What an interesting . . . !
Wow!

Disagreeing
Do you think so? I think . . . .
I don't agree.
I don't think so.
It's different in my country.
Not really.

GRAMMAR EXTENSION *Present participles*

Add *-ing:*	go	→	go**ing**
	work	→	work**ing**
Drop *e* and add *-ing:*	live	→	liv**ing**
Double the final consonant and add *-ing:*	get	→	get**ting**
	shop	→	shop**ping**

6 HOW OFTEN DO YOU EXERCISE?

KEY VOCABULARY

Nouns
Sports and fitness activities
aerobics
basketball
bicycling
football
jogging
racquetball
Rollerblading
soccer
swimming
tennis
weight training
yoga

Other
classmate
couch potato
fitness freak
free time
(fitness) program
sports fanatic
teen(ager)

Pronoun
nothing

Adjectives
good (at sports/for you)
fit
in (great) shape
middle-aged
old
popular
regular

Verbs
exercise
guess
keep
learn
lift (weights)
play (a sport)
stay
take (a walk)
work out

Adverb
hard
just (= only)
sometime
too

Prepositions
in (my free time)
for (a walk)
like (that)

Interjection
say

EXPRESSIONS

Talking about routines
How often do you . . . ?
Three times a week/day/month.
I don't . . . very often.
Do you ever . . . ?
How much time do you spend . . . ?
Around two hours a day.

Talking about abilities
How well do you . . . ?
Pretty well.
Not very well.
How good are you at . . . ?
I'm pretty good, I guess.
Not too good.

Asking for more information
What else . . . ?

Expressing surprise
You're kidding!

Agreeing
All right.
No problem.

GRAMMAR EXTENSION Placement of adverbs of frequency

Questions
Is he usually at the gym after work?
be + subject + adverb

Statements
He is usually at the gym after work.
subject + *be* + adverb

He isn't usually there on weekends.
subject + negative *be* + adverb

Questions
Does he usually go to the gym after work?
does + subject + adverb + verb

Statements
He usually goes to the gym after work.
subject + adverb + verb

He usually doesn't go on weekends.
subject + adverb + *doesn't* + verb

Always usually goes between *don't / doesn't* and the main verb.

He doesn't always go to the gym on weekends.
subject + *doesn't* + adverb + verb

7 WE HAD A GREAT TIME!

KEY VOCABULARY

Nouns
car
city
concert
(the) country
dancing
dishes
drive
housework
lake
neighbor
noise
party
picnic
trip
weather

Pronouns
anything
everyone
someone

Adjectives
all
boring
broke
cool
difficult
foggy
special
terrific

Verbs
baby-sit
complain
drive
enjoy
go shopping
have (someone) over
have (a[n] . . . time/
  [a lot of] fun)
invite (someone) out
see
snow
take (a day off)
work on

Adverbs
Time expressions
all day/month/year
all the time
as usual
last night/summer/weekend
the whole time
yesterday

Other
also
around
away
unfortunately

Prepositions
in (the country)
on (a trip/business/vacation)
over (the weekend)

EXPRESSIONS

Talking about past activities
Did you go out on Saturday?
What did you do . . . ?
How did you spend . . . ?
Where did you go . . . ?
What time did you go . . . ?
How long were you . . . ?

Giving opinions about past experiences
How did you like . . . ?/
How was . . . ?
  It was . . . . /I really enjoyed it.
What was the best thing about . . . ?
  It's difficult to say.
Was the . . . OK?

Making and responding to suggestions
Why don't you (just) . . . ?
  But then what would I do . . . ?

GRAMMAR EXTENSION *Sentences about the weather*

How was the weather?

it + *be*
It was cool/cold/freezing.
  warm/hot.
  sunny/clear.
  cloudy/rainy.
  windy/foggy.

it + verb
It rained/snowed.

8 HOW DO YOU LIKE THE NEIGHBORHOOD?

KEY VOCABULARY

Nouns
Neighborhood/ Community places
apartment (building)
aquarium
bank
barber shop
bookstore
cafe
coffee shop
dance club
drugstore
gas station
grocery store
hotel
laundromat
library
(science) museum
park
pay phone
post office
shopping center
stationery store
street
travel agency

Other
air
bedroom
book
card
crime
dining room
idea
kitchen
living room
ocean
paper (= stationery)
pollution
public transportation
suburbs
traffic
unemployment
water

Adjectives
busy
clean
close
convenient
important
low
near
quiet
safe

Verbs
borrow
dry
happen
make (a reservation)
move in
trade (places)
wash

Adverbs
downtown
nearby

Prepositions
in (the shopping center/ your neighborhood)
on (Pine Street/Third Avenue)

Interjections
by the way
in fact
of course

EXPRESSIONS

Asking for and giving locations
Is there a/an . . . around here?
 Yes, there is. There's one . . . .
 No, there isn't, but there's one . . . .
 Sorry, I don't know.
Are there any . . . near here?
 Yes, there are. There are some . . . .
 No, there aren't, but there are some . . . .
 I'm not sure, but I think . . . .

Complaining
That's the trouble.

Asking about quantities
How much . . . is there?
 There's a lot/a little/none.
 There isn't much/any.
How many . . . are there?
 There are a lot/a few/none.
 There aren't many/any.

Giving opinions
I bet . . . .

GRAMMAR EXTENSION

1. Countable and uncountable nouns

Countable

Singular	Plural
a bookstore	(**some**) bookstores
an apartment	(**some**) apartments

Uncountable

Singular	Plural
(**some**) traffic	–
(**some**) noise	–

2. *Some* and *any*

Questions
Is there **a** bookstore?
Are there **any** bookstores?

Statements
There are **some** bookstores.

Negatives
There aren't **any** bookstores.

Questions
Is there traffic?
any traffic?

Statements
There is **some** traffic.

Negatives
There isn't **any** traffic.

9 WHAT DOES HE LOOK LIKE?

KEY VOCABULARY

Nouns
beard
centimeter (cm)
contact lenses
couch
couple
eye
fashion
foot/feet
glasses
guy
hair
hand
height
length
man
mustache
person
T-shirt
window
woman

Adjectives
bald
blond
curly
good-looking
handsome
khaki
serious-looking
short
straight
tall

Verbs
ask for
change
miss
sit
stand
wear

Adverbs
ago
fairly
pretty
quite

Prepositions
in (a T-shirt and jeans/his thirties)
on (the couch)
to (the left [of])
with (red hair)

EXPRESSIONS

Greeting someone
Good afternoon.
Good to see you.

Offering help
Can I help you?
Yes, I'm looking for . . . .

Asking about someone's appearance
What does she look like?
How old is she?
What color is her hair/are her eyes?
How tall is she?

Identifying people
Which one is Judy?
She's the one talking to Tom.
Who's Brian?
He's the man with curly blond hair/in jeans/ behind the couch.

Expressing intention
I'll go and . . . .

Expressing regret
I'm afraid . . .

Hesitating
Let's see.

Confirming information
Are you . . . ?
Yes, that's right.

GRAMMAR EXTENSION Be *and* have *to describe someone*

be + adjective
I**'m** 18.
He**'s** bald.
She**'s** tall.
They**'re** medium height.

have + noun
I **have** brown hair.
He **has** a mustache and a beard
She **has** blue eyes.
They **have** curly black hair.

10 HAVE YOU EVER RIDDEN A CAMEL?

KEY VOCABULARY

Nouns
accident
appointment
audience
bird
breakfast
bungee jumping
camel
camera
(body-building) competition
(a) couple (of)
fire
fish
grocery shopping
hill
kiwi (fruit)
laundry
magic
magician
(goat's) milk
motorcycle
mountain
pastime
pleasure
riverboat
skiing
sports car
truck
wallet
way
wedding
(a) while
white-water rafting
(rice) wine

Pronouns
several
something

Adjectives
every
exciting
incredible
raw
several
unusual
valuable
wonderful

Verbs
call
clean
climb
decide
drink
eat
hike
jog
lose
make (your bed)
ride
try

Adverbs
actually
already
lately
once
recently
today
twice
yet

Prepositions
for (a while)
in (a long time)

Conjunction
because

EXPRESSIONS

Exchanging information about past experiences
Have you ever . . . ?
Yes, I have./No, I haven't.

Giving a suggestion
You should . . . .

Agreeing
Sure.

Checking and sharing information
The magician?
That's right.
I hear . . . .

GRAMMAR EXTENSION *Time expressions*

With present perfect

Time expressions refer to indefinite times in the past.

I've **already** seen that show.
I've seen it **twice**.
I haven't seen it **yet**.
I haven't been to the movies **in a long time**.

With past tense

Time expressions refer to specific times in the past.

I saw it **last night**.
I saw it **yesterday**.
I saw it **last Friday**.
I went to the movies **about a month ago**.

11 IT'S A VERY EXCITING CITY!

KEY VOCABULARY

Nouns
Seasons
fall
spring
summer
winter

Other
arrival
beach
departure
harbor
hometown
(flea) market
million
nightlife
tourist
visitor

Pronoun
you (= anyone)

Adjectives
beautiful
cold
crowded
dangerous
dirty
friendly
hot
humid
modern
relaxing
stressful
ugly

Verbs
Modals
can
should

Other
hate

Adverb
anytime

Prepositions
at (the beach)
in (the fall)
on (the street)

Conjunctions
however
though

EXPRESSIONS

Describing something
What's . . . like?
It's . . . , but it's not too . . . .
It's . . . , and it's . . . .

Asking for a favor
Can you . . . ?
Yes, I can./Sure I can.
No, I can't.

Asking for and giving suggestions
What should I . . . ?
You should . . . .
You shouldn't . . . .
Should I . . . ?
Yes, you should./
No, you shouldn't.

Talking about advisability
What can you do?
You can . . . .
You can't . . . .

GRAMMAR EXTENSION *Sentences with* and, but, however, though

These sentences mean the same: They contrast something good *(a beautiful city)* and something bad *(very hot).*

This is a beautiful city, **but** it's very hot in the summer.
It's very hot in the summer, **however**.
It's very hot in the summer, **though**.

In this sentence, the conjunction *and* adds information.

This is a beautiful city, **and** there's always a lot to do.

12 *IT REALLY WORKS!*

KEY VOCABULARY

Nouns
Health problems
backache
burn
cold
cough
dry skin
fever
flu
headache
hiccups
insect bite
insomnia
muscle
pain
sore throat
stomachache
stress
sunburn
toothache

Containers and medicines
antacid
aspirin
bandage
bottle
box
can
cold tablets
cough drops
(anti-itch/skin) cream
(eye) drops
heating pad
lotion
ointment
package
sleeping pills
spray
tissue
tube
vitamin (C)

Other
chicken stock
dentist
garlic
liquid
meat
medicine cabinet
pepper
pharmacist
remedy
rest
slice

Adjectives
excellent
folk
half
helpful
lots of
sore
tired
useful

Verbs
Modals
could
may

Other
chop up
cut
get (a cold)
put
rest
take (medicine/
something for . . .)
tie
suggest
work (= succeed)

Prepositions
in (bed)
under (cold water)

EXPRESSIONS

Talking about health problems
How are you?
Not so good. I have . . . .
That's too bad.

Offering and accepting assistance
Can/May I help you?
Yes, please. Could/Can/May I have . . . ?
Here you are.
Thanks a lot.

Asking for and giving advice
What should you do . . . ?
It's helpful/a good idea to . . . .

Asking for and giving suggestions
What do you have/suggest for . . . ?
Try/I suggest/You should get . . . .

Expressing dislike
Ugh!

GRAMMAR EXTENSION *Sentences with* have got *to talk about health problems*

What's the matter?	**I've got** a bad cold. She**'s got** the flu.	*Contractions* I have = **I've** She has = She**'s**

13 MAY I TAKE YOUR ORDER, PLEASE?

KEY VOCABULARY

Nouns
Food and beverages
bread
broth
(chocolate) cake
(clam) chowder
(cup of) coffee
cole slaw
cucumber
dessert
dressing
flavor
(french) fries
(mixed) greens
hamburger
ice cream
lemon
main dish
meal
meatballs
milk
pasta
(apple) pie
potato
rice
salad
salmon
seafood
spaghetti
soda
(onion) soup
steak
(iced) tea
tomato
turkey
vegetable
vinaigrette

Other
customer
order
tip
waiter
waitress

Pronoun
all

Adjectives
baked
bland
delicious
ethnic
fried
greasy
grilled
healthy
mashed
rich
roast
salty
spicy

Verbs
Modals
will
would

Other
bring
go back
order

Adverbs
a bit
(not) at all
for now
right away

Preposition
with (lemon)

EXPRESSIONS

Expressing feelings
I'm crazy about . . . .
I'm (not) in the mood for . . . .

Agreeing and disagreeing
I like . . . .
  So do I./I do, too.
I don't like . . . .
  Neither do I./I don't either.
I'm crazy about . . . .
  So am I./I am, too.
I'm not in the mood for . . . .
  Neither am I./I'm not either.
I can . . . .
  So can I./I can, too.
I can't . . . .
  Neither can I./I can't either.

Ordering in a restaurant
May I take your order, please?/
What would you like?
  I'd like/I'll have a/an/the . . . .
What kind of . . . would you like?
  I'd like/I'll have . . . , please.
Would you like anything else?
  Yes, please. I'd like . . . .
  No, thank you. That will be all.

GRAMMAR EXTENSION Polite requests

Imperative
Please bring me a glass of water.

Questions with can/could/will/would
Can you please bring me a glass of water?
Could . . . .
Will . . . .
Would . . . .

14 THE BIGGEST AND THE BEST!

KEY VOCABULARY

Nouns
Geography
canyon
cliff
continent
desert
"down under" (= Australia and New Zealand)
farm
field
forest
plain
plateau
(coral) reef
river
sea
swamp
valley
volcano
waterfall

Measurements
degree (Fahrenheit/Celsius)
kilometer
meter
(square) mile
temperature

Other
artist
attraction
butter
feather
town

Adjectives
deep
far
heavy
high
located
lucky
mountainous

Verbs
get up (to)
go down (to)

Prepositions
in (the mountains/the world)
of (the three)
on (Bali)

EXPRESSIONS

Talking about distance and measurements
How far is . . . from . . . ?
It's about . . . kilometers/miles.
How big is . . . ?
It's . . . square kilometers.
How high is . . . ?
It's . . . meters/feet high.
How deep is (the) . . . ?
It's . . . meters deep.
How long is (the) . . . ?
It's . . . kilometers long.
How hot is . . . in the summer?
It gets up to . . . degrees.
How cold is . . . in the winter?
It goes down to . . . degrees.

Making comparisons
Which country is larger, . . . or . . . ?
. . . is larger than . . . .
Which country is the largest: . . . , . . . , or . . . ?
. . . is the largest of the three.
What is the most beautiful . . . in the world?
I think . . . is the most beautiful.

GRAMMAR EXTENSION *Superlative of adjectives*

Adjectives with -est

Add *-est:*	high	→ high**est**
Add *-st:*	large	→ large**st**
Drop *y* and add *-iest:*	dry	→ dr**iest**
Double the final consonant and add *-est:*	big	→ big**gest**

Adjectives with most
most + adjective: **most** famous
most mountainous

See the appendix at the back of the book for a list of adjectives.

15 I'M GOING TO SEE A MUSICAL.

KEY VOCABULARY

Nouns
(comedy) act
(leisure) activity
address
amusement park
barbecue
cafeteria
(telephone) call
dictionary
(craft) fair
(arts/crafts) festival
gathering
handout
hockey
meeting
message
monument
musical
plan
spectator
(tennis) tournament
turn

Adjectives
canceled
historic
live

Verbs
finish
give
open
pick (someone) up
plan
return
speak

Adverbs
in
overtime
tomorrow

Prepositions
at (college)
till (7:00)

Conjunction
that

EXPRESSIONS

Talking about plans
What are you doing tonight?
  I'm going . . . .
Are you doing anything tomorrow/ tonight?
  No, I'm not.
What is he going to do tonight?
  He's going to . . . .
Is he going to . . . tomorrow night?
  Yes, he is.

Apologizing and giving reasons
I'm sorry, but I can't go.
I'm working late.

Accepting and refusing invitations
Would you like to . . . ?/
Do you want to . . . ?
  I'd love to.
  Oh, sorry, I can't.

Making a business call
Good morning, ...
  Hello. May I speak to . . . , please?
. . .'s not in. Can I take a message?
  Yes, please. This is . . . . Would you ask . . . to call me? My number is . . . .
I'll give . . . the message.
  Thank you. Good-bye.

Leaving and taking messages
Can/May I take a message?
  Please tell . . . (that) . . . .
  Please ask . . . to . . . .
  Would/Could you tell . . . (that) . . . ?
  Would/Could you ask . . . to . . . ?

GRAMMAR EXTENSION Future sentences

With be going to

The verb *be* is always used in the *be going to* form – never in the present continuous.

Where **are** you **going to be** tomorrow?
  I'm going to be at home.

With present continuous

Arrive, come, go, leave, and *stay* are usually used in the present continuous.

We**'re arriving** tomorrow.
  coming
  going
  leaving
  staying

16 A CHANGE FOR THE BETTER!

KEY VOCABULARY

Nouns
biology
course
degree
(environmental) education
forestry
graduation
hairstyle
kid
life/lives
(student) loan
photo album
weight

Adjectives
dressed up
easy
outgoing
own
successful

Verbs
become
bring about
date
dress
fall (in love)
grow
hope
join
pay off
quit
retire
smoke
start
type

Adverbs
anymore
differently
for ages

Prepositions
at (an early age)
into (a new apartment)

EXPRESSIONS

Exchanging personal information
How have you been?
  Pretty good.
How are you?
  I'm doing really well.

Describing changes
You've really changed!
  I'm married now.
  I don't wear glasses anymore.
  My job is easier (now).
  I'm heavier (than before).
  I got divorced.
  I've grown a mustache.

Talking about plans for the future
I'm (not) going to . . . .
I (don't) plan to . . . .
I (don't) want to . . . .
I hope to . . . .
I'd like/love to . . . .

GRAMMAR EXTENSION *Review: Wh-questions*

What's your name?
What do you do?
What time do you get up?
What kind of music do you like?
What do you look like?
What color are your eyes?
What are you like?
What are you doing these days?
What did you do last night?
What do you think of Brad Pitt?

When do you get home?
When are you leaving?

Where are you from?
Where do you work?
Where did you go yesterday?
Where were you?
Which jeans do you like better,
  the light ones or the dark ones?
Which one is Tom?

Who is that?
Who's your favorite actress?
Who did you go out with last night?
Who's Sarah?

How do you like your job?
How do you spend your day?
How did you spend your last birthday?
How was your trip?

How much is that blouse?
How much crime is there in your city?
How many restaurants are there in your neighborhood?

How often do you exercise?
How well do you play?
How good are you at sports?
How long do you spend working out?
How long were you away?
How much time do you spend at the gym?
How old are you?
How long is your hair?
How tall are you?

Why don't you buy a new car?

Appendix

COUNTRIES AND NATIONALITIES

This is a partial list of countries, many of which are presented in this book.

Country	Nationality
Argentina	Argentine
Australia	Australian
Austria	Austrian
Brazil	Brazilian
Bolivia	Bolivian
Canada	Canadian
Chile	Chilean
China	Chinese
Colombia	Colombian
Costa Rica	Costa Rican
Ecuador	Ecuadorian
Egypt	Egyptian
England	English
France	French
Germany	German
Greece	Greek
Hungary	Hungarian
India	Indian
Indonesia	Indonesian
Ireland	Irish
Italy	Italian
Japan	Japanese
Korea	Korean
Lebanon	Lebanese
Malaysia	Malaysian
Mexico	Mexican
Morocco	Moroccan
New Zealand	New Zealander
the Philippines	Filipino
Poland	Polish
Russia	Russian
Singapore	Singaporean
Spain	Spanish
Switzerland	Swiss
Thailand	Thai
Turkey	Turkish
Peru	Peruvian
the United Kingdom	British
the United States	American
Uruguay	Uruguayan

NUMBERS

0 zero	1 one	2 two	3 three	4 four	5 five	6 six	7 seven	8 eight
9 nine	10 ten	11 eleven	12 twelve	13 thirteen	14 fourteen	15 fifteen	16 sixteen	17 seventeen
18 eighteen	19 nineteen	20 twenty	21 twenty-one	22 twenty-two	30 thirty	40 forty	50 fifty	60 sixty
70 seventy	80 eighty	90 ninety	100 one hundred (a hundred)			1,000 one thousand (a thousand)		

COMPARATIVE AND SUPERLATIVE ADJECTIVES

1. Adjective with *-er* and *-est*

big	dirty	high	old	tall
busy	dry	hot	pretty	ugly
cheap	easy	large	quiet	warm
clean	fast	light	safe	wet
close	friendly	long	scary	young
cold	funny	mild	short	
cool	great	new	slow	
deep	heavy	nice	small	

2. Adjectives with *more* and *most*

attractive	exciting	outgoing
beautiful	expensive	popular
boring	famous	relaxing
crowded	important	stressful
dangerous	interesting	difficult
delicious		

3. Irregular adjectives

good → better → best
bad → worse → the worst